100 IDEAS
FOR LESSON PLANNING

CONTINUUM ONE HUNDREDS SERIES

100 IDEAS FOR LESSON PLANNING

Anthony Haynes

continuum

Continuum International Publishing Group
The Tower Building   80 Maiden Lane, Suite 704
11 York Road   New York, NY 10038
SE1 7NX

www.continuumbooks.com

British Library Cataloguing-in-Publication Data
A catalogue record for this book is available from the British Library.

ISBN: 0826483089 (paperback)

Library of Congress Cataloguing-in-Publication Data
A catalog record for this book is available from the Library of Congress.

Typeset by Ben Cracknell Studios | www.benstudios.co.uk
Printed and bound in Great Britain by Ashford Colour Press, Gosport, Hampshire

CONTENTS

SECTION 4   The two BIG ideas – progression and differentiation

SECTION 5   The role of language

DEDICATION
To Cathy Carpenter, Mary Palmer, Emma Knill
and Sam Allen – former pupils who have become
teachers themselves.

This book covers both planning and aspects of
lesson *preparation* (creating resources, for example).
I decided against '100 Ideas for Lesson Planning and
Preparation' as a title because it sounds clunky. I hope,
however, that the inclusion of preparation as well as
planning causes no surprise. I doubt that it will – for
teachers, planning and preparation tend to go together
(something like hand and glove).

I should say a word about special educational needs.
I have dealt with this topic only in a general way. I have
not included information about particular special
needs. That would require a different book.

In preparing this book I have been very surprised at
how few good sources there are for ideas about lesson
planning. The subject accounts for a surprisingly small
proportion of educational publishing. I hope this book
goes some way towards plugging the gap in provision.

My thanks are again due to my editor, the
constructive but scrupulous Christina Garbutt.

Introducing planning

IDEA

1

BENEFITING FROM PLANNING

Few will doubt that there is a point to lesson planning. If you've had much experience of standing in front of classes without a lesson plan, you'll know how unsatisfactory that can feel.

But let's be more precise. Planning boosts confidence. By taking care of certain questions in advance – what, how, and with what you're going to teach – you free yourself to concentrate on the class in front of you and the business of actually teaching.

Planning gives you something you can communicate – to pupils ('In this lesson you will learn . . .') and to colleagues, especially support staff (see Idea 77). The provision of teaching assistants is a major item in most schools' budget, yet some teachers fail to make best use of them by not explaining lessons beforehand. Lack of planning wastes, and demotivates, support staff.

The most important point, however, is that lesson planning enables you to optimize things. Without planning, you may find you're able to get by or even produce an adequate lesson, but you'll not be teaching with maximum effect. When planning lessons, therefore, ask yourself not 'What can I teach them?' but 'What's the *best* thing I can teach them?', not 'How can I teach this?' but 'What's the *best* way I can teach it?'

It is natural when one first goes into teaching to think in terms of the following sequence:

Planning ⇨ Lesson ⇨ Assessment

Natural, but not right.

After you have planned and taught the lesson and then assessed your pupils' work, you need to use the information that you have gained from assessment to inform your planning of the next lesson that you teach that class (see Idea 33). You need to:

1 Consider what the assessment data tell you in general about the lesson that you have just taught. Are there, for example, points that have not been well understood and which you need to cover again?
2 Decide how you will give marked work back to pupils and encourage them to learn from your assessment.
3 Consider whether the assessment information on particular pupils suggests you need to give special consideration to the way you teach them (see Idea 33).

You also need to consider whether, in the light of the assessment data, you should change the lesson the next time you teach it, which may be next year (see Idea 85).

There needs, therefore, to be a further arrow in the sequence above, leading back from assessment to planning. Learning to see planning as part of a cycle of teaching and learning is one of the most important steps on the road to becoming a fully developed teacher.

THE DIFFERENCE BETWEEN 'PLANNING' AND PLANNING

When I was doing my teaching practice I planned each lesson very fully. I was given time off-timetable to do so. When I moved on to become a newly qualified teacher (NQT), I continued to plan lessons carefully. As both a trainee and an NQT I was in any case required to keep records of lessons.

Every year after that my plans proceeded to become less and less explicit. I still wrote notes in advance for every lesson. Often, however, they were very brief – a simple label for each main part of the lesson, some point about a particular pupil ('Chase Simon for his homework'). I told myself that I didn't need fleshed-out plans because I knew the courses, knew what I was doing, had taught most of the lessons before.

Then I changed schools and gained responsibility. The twin stimuli forced me to re-evaluate my practice and to think afresh. I reverted to writing explicit plans for each lesson. I noticed immediately that my teaching sharpened up. In particular, I started redesigning lessons that I'd taught many times before. And I started giving much more forethought to the needs of individual pupils.

There are two points to this parable. The first is simply that it pays to plan each lesson:

o fully;
o explicitly;
o in writing.

The second is that the benefits of doing so apply as much to the seasoned professional as to the novice.

There is a large quantity of teaching material and lesson plans available to teachers through commercially published resource packs and the Internet (see Idea 92). In England the Government kindly provides detailed plans for lessons on numeracy and literacy via its official strategies.

Though such resources can be useful, they share a common problem. Their originators typically pay little attention to context. Teachers who contribute their favourite plans to websites, for example, usually say nothing about the context in which the plans were first developed. And, arguably, the whole point of the various government strategies in England has been to pretend that context didn't matter.

Ever tried moving schools? Sometimes a lesson will work in the same way, and with equal success, in more than one school. But often it will not. Differences concerning pupils, the curriculum, the tradition and ethos of the school, its architecture, and the local community often mean that the same lesson produces different outcomes.

At the beginning of my career I taught in a self-styled Progressive community college, then in a mixed ex-secondary modern school, then in a former boys' grammar. I could hardly fail to notice that my standard lessons tended to play differently in each. For the same reason I do not suppose anyone in England has been surprised that the Government's 'one size fits all' strategies have, despite desperate attempts to massage the assessment results, failed to achieve their targets.

The key principle that emerges is that however attractive an idea for a lesson and however enthusiastically it is recommended, you always have to consider what kind of adaptation is needed for the circumstances you work in. Whether you are preparing a lesson you have taught elsewhere or adapting a plan borrowed from another source, it pays to ask: What are the salient points about the context of this lesson? How do I need to revise the plan to accommodate them?

YOUR OWN STYLE

Every now and then you hear someone – a colleague or a trainer – say something like, 'This always goes down well' or, 'Kids love doing this'. Thank goodness, you think, something I can count on at last. So you take the idea back to your classroom and, full of hope, launch the lesson.

Sometimes the lesson does indeed go well. Very early in my career someone recommended Sandy Brownjohn's ideas for teaching writing and they provided me with numerous successful lessons.

On the other hand, sometimes the idea sinks. For example, many teachers have assured me that children find the history of language fascinating – the derivations of words, their changes in meaning, all that kind of thing. I have more than a passing interest in the subject myself. Yet I do not recall ever teaching a really successful lesson on that topic. Somehow the supply of fascination that other teachers had tapped into with their pupils always got turned off whenever I tried it!

Questions of individual style are inescapable. This is probably no bad thing – but they do need to be accommodated by your planning. Consider, therefore: What is your style? How can you adapt your planning to suit your style? How can you customize plans that you have borrowed from colleagues, books or websites? It's easier to adapt the plan than the style.

You need to plan on three different timescales: the long term, medium term and short term.

Long-term planning covers at least a complete school year. To plan over this length of time you will need to consider the (a) continuity and progression, (b) balance and breadth and (c) coherence of the curriculum.

For the first of these considerations, ask yourself to what extent each stage of the curriculum (i) reinforces what pupils have learnt before, (ii) builds on and develops their learning, (iii) introduces new elements and (iv) prepares pupils for future learning.

For the second, ask yourself whether (i) a wide enough range of learning is provided, (ii) there are any unintended gaps and (iii) each area of learning is covered in sufficient depth.

For the third, ask yourself how well the curriculum 'hangs together'. In particular, are cross-curricular issues (e.g. study skills) covered adequately or have any slipped down the cracks?

When considering the coherence of the curriculum, you need to look at learning from the pupil's point of view. Usually each teacher experiences only part of the curriculum – a particular subject or year group. The people who experience the entire curriculum are the pupils.

LONG-TERM PLANNING

SCHEMES OF WORK

The cornerstone of medium-term planning is the scheme of work. Schemes of work occupy a crucial position in teachers' planning. There is no doubt that good teachers think in terms of schemes of work. Learning to think in that way, rather than purely in terms of individual lessons, is one of the most fundamental steps in a teacher's development.

What should be in a scheme of work? Even a complete novice will include subject content and the learning activities to be performed by pupils. Most teachers soon learn to supplement these with a specification of the aims of the lesson, the resources required and the forms of assessment to be used.

To develop expertise in planning, however, it is necessary to go further. You need to ask questions such as: How will you supplement your aims with a list of objectives? What do pupils need to learn and what support do they need? What is the scope of the work? What pedagogical methods will you use? What kind and level of work do you expect? What homework will you set? How will you differentiate the work? How will it contribute to pupils' progression? What use will you make of any ancillary staff? What risks are involved? How will you evaluate the scheme of work?

A checklist for a 'Perfect Plan' is given in the Appendix.

Needs, aims and objectives

ANALYSIS OF NEEDS

An analysis of pupils' needs is a frequently (perhaps even routinely) overlooked stage in devising a scheme of work. The problem is exacerbated by official curricula imposed by government, which simply make assumptions about what pupils need without any knowledge of the pupils themselves. Unfortunately, if we ignore pupils' needs there is likely to be a disconnect between our curriculum and their learning.

Pupils have two kinds of needs. First, there are the general ones that provide the preconditions for education – the need for such things as security, comfort and dignity. Second, there are learning needs – provision for special educational needs such as dyslexia, for example, or remedial action to help pupils make good any gaps in their knowledge from earlier parts of the curriculum.

There has been much debate in the philosophy of education about what constitutes a need and how needs may be distinguished from other things, such as wants and desires. One might argue, for example, that not all of the 'needs' mentioned above are genuine needs – discomfort, for example, does not necessarily make learning impossible.

From the point of view of routine planning, however, we need not worry overmuch about such distinctions. If something facilitates learning, then it is desirable to incorporate it in our planning, whether or not it is a genuine need. We do, however, need to keep one distinction in mind, namely that between education and social welfare. In our role as educators our interest in pupils' needs is from the point of view of their learning. Education, after all, is often what empowers people to satisfy their needs for themselves.

To assess pupils' needs you need first to consult assessment data, the special needs register and pupil records (including such matters as health, attendance and behaviour) in order to identify any unusual needs. Then consider how you can satisfy (or at least allow for) such needs in your schemes of work.

Aims and objectives, though often spoken of in the same breath, need to be distinguished. Aims are more general and tend to be more long term and less measurable. If before a driving lesson you asked a driving instructor what s/he was hoping to achieve, the response might be, 'I want to teach A to drive' or, 'I want to teach A how to change gear'. The former answer articulates an aim, the latter an objective.

There are two approaches to the articulation of aims in schemes of work – the cynical and the professional. The Cynic thinks, 'I don't need to think about aims, I'm sure what I'm teaching is valuable and anyway I have to teach it because it's in the syllabus. But for bureaucratic purposes I have to write down some aims. However, since aims are general and difficult to measure, I can get away with some vague phrase that shows I'm trying to teach something that everybody agrees is a Good Thing.' So the Cynic writes as an aim something like (in the case of a sequence of history lessons, say) 'To show how life in Victorian times differs from life today'.

The Professional thinks, 'Defining my aims helps me to stand back for a moment from the hurly-burly of setting tests, giving out worksheets, marking homework, etc. I can clarify, or remind myself, what all this activity is for and why it's worth doing.' In fact, writing a set of aims provides teachers with a chance to reconnect with their educational idealism (which is often what brought them into teaching in the first place). Even if the Professional writes exactly the same as the Cynic, s/he will – because s/he believes in the aim – use it as a principle for constructing the rest of the scheme of work and hence
be more likely to achieve it.

Ask yourself what you *really* want to achieve.

SELF-ASSESSMENT OF AIMS

This is an idea I hit on when learning to teach adult classes and then used with (quite senior) classes in school at the beginning of their courses. Make a numbered list of the aims that pupils might have for the course you are teaching them. For example:

1 Achieve a qualification.
2 Get the best grade at the end of the course.
3 Progress to a further course.
4 Muddle through.
5 Find out more about [a specified area of the subject].
6 I have no specific aims.

At the end of the list leave room for pupils to write in their own aims.

Now ask them to put the aims into rank order. Because of its abstractness, the task can be quite difficult to do. Idea 66, however, provides some ways of making it more concrete.

Once you have collated the results you can have a discussion about the aims themselves, the differences of opinion within the class, your own aims, and so on. Quite apart from the discussion itself, the exercise shows where your pupils are starting from (however disappointing that may be!) and avoids you having to double guess.

Setting objectives in your lesson planning has a number of benefits. It helps you to decide precisely what it is you are trying to achieve and to design your lessons accordingly. It also helps you to explain to pupils what it is you want them to do and to learn. And it makes it easier to communicate to colleagues, parents, and others what you are doing and why you are doing it.

Some objectives are more useful than others. The best objectives do three things at once. They specify:

1 what pupils should be able to do as a result of their learning;
2 in what context or under what conditions they should be able to perform those actions;
3 at what level pupils are expected to perform.

When you have written a draft of your learning objectives, use the above as a checklist to see whether they need tightening up. In my experience, most teachers' objectives specify (1) better than they do (2) and (3).

THE RATIONALE OF OBJECTIVES

Here is a checklist of the qualities an objective should have. The initial letters of each item form the (unfortunate, but memorable) mnemonic 'SCAM'. The ideal objective will be:

○ *S*pecific in terms of (a) what is to be learnt and (b) the time within which it is to be learnt;
○ *C*apable of assessment;
○ *A*chievable;
○ *M*anageable in the context you are working in.

Some of these qualities are inherent in the concept of an objective, others are desirable because they help to motivate your pupils and preserve your morale.

You need to ensure that your learning objectives result in pupils doing things that can be observed – otherwise you have no way of assessing whether the objectives have been met. It helps, therefore, to phrase your objectives with this point in mind. The key words will be the verbs you use to describe the desired outcomes.

Try to avoid vague words such as 'understand'. If you say that your objective is for 'pupils to understand X' it is difficult to know whether you have succeeded. What does understanding look like? Seek to use verbs that refer to observable actions on the part of your pupils.

You might specify, for example, that pupils will: apply, arrange, assess, attempt, build, calculate, challenge, chart, check, choose, compare, compose, construct, contrast, count, correct, criticize, demonstrate, describe, design, disprove, draft, draw, enact, estimate, explain, evaluate, find, forecast, gauge, hypothesize, identify, illustrate, indicate, judge, label, list, locate, make, match, measure, model, note, observe, operate, organize, outline, perform, plan, play, predict, prepare, produce, programme, prove, quantify, recite, record, recognize, rehearse, repeat, report, rewrite, select, sketch, solve, state, summarize, test, tell, use, verify or work X.

Over a period of time the learning objectives you set can start to feel very samey. K. Paul Kasambira suggests thinking in terms of three different types of objective.

First, there are 'hunting' objectives. These are to be found when everyone concerned knows precisely what the teacher is after. 'Write a one-page dialogue using speech marks correctly' is an example. Kasambira suggests 'behavioural' as a synonym for 'hunting' in this context.

Second, there are 'fishing' objectives. These occur when it is less certain what sort of outcome the teacher expects or how the outcome may be measured. 'Appreciate the structure of a novel' is an example. Kasambira suggests 'affective' as a synonym for 'fishing' here.

Third, there are expressive objectives. These relate to pupils' skill in expression, for example, writing a letter of protest to a newspaper, giving a speech in support of a policy, designing a poster to communicate a message.

You can use Kasambira's typology first to analyse the objectives you have been setting so far and, second, to help broaden your repertoire.

Ideas 11–14 are based on the assumption that learning objectives form a useful part of lesson planning. Some educators, however, argue that using objectives – either because of the objectives themselves or the use to which they are put – can be limiting or even harmful.

Objectives are based on the notion that education is observable and measurable. This may be true for some forms of learning, such as the technique for throwing a javelin. The notion is most applicable when teaching takes the form of training. But it applies less well to other forms of education. We might want our pupils to, say, appreciate the structure of a symphony, marvel at the complexity of the human body or harmonize with nature. Such outcomes are less demonstrable – yet are often highly valued. An insistence on objectives can drive out such forms of education.

Education can also be heuristic. A teacher using discovery methods in group drama, for example, may from experience be confident that *some* outcomes of value will result, without being certain in advance what form they will take. The teacher will recognize such outcomes when s/he sees them. Or a pupil might lead a class discussion in a completely unanticipated, but nevertheless valuable, direction. Surely the teacher doesn't want to prohibit such discussion purely because it doesn't accord with predetermined objectives?

It is important to remember in your planning that learning objectives are neither all-important nor capable of encapsulating all types of learning.

THE LIMITATIONS OF LEARNING OBJECTIVES

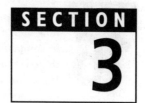

Learning

BEHAVIOURIST LEARNING

Psychologists have developed various theories to explain how humans learn. To some extent these theories are in competition with each other. Among psychologists there is much discussion about their relative merits. Educators tend to take a pragmatic view. Each of the major theories may have some truth in it. It may be that we learn different things in different ways at different times.

One such theory, associated (more or less accurately) with such psychologists as Pavlov, Thorndike, and Skinner, is behaviourism. Behaviourists tend to see learning in mechanistic terms as a chain reaction of stimuli and responses. Think of a game of snooker. The movement of the cue sets the white ball in motion, which in turn sets other balls in motion by impacting upon them. One may compare this to our action of stopping (= response) when we see a red light (= stimulus). What counts at a crossroads is whether or not we stop – the question of what mental state(s) we are in when we do so is (at least according to some versions of behaviourism) neither more important nor more observable than the mental state of the snooker ball. The difference between snooker balls and humans is merely that one can condition the latter through rewards and punishment – punishing drivers for jumping red lights might make them less likely to do so again.

Behaviourist planning is most useful where stimuli are clearly distinguishable and classifiable. When I was in the sixth form, for instance, I was taught that (but not *why*) if the examiner posed a general question, I should make my answer specific – and vice versa. That's a good example of behaviourist teaching.

Identify the places where behaviourist teaching is most practicable in your subject. Consider in particular:

○ Which parts of your lessons lend themselves to thinking in terms of stimulus and response?
○ Where do assessment criteria require only certain *outcomes* rather than levels of *understanding*?

Cognitivist psychology, which was developed by thinkers such as John Dewey and Jerome Bruner, is very different from behaviourism (see Idea 16). Cognitivists pay a good deal of attention to what is going on inside learners' minds, especially the questions of how learners understand things and assign meanings to them.

Cognitivism is founded on the idea that learners construct mental pictures of the world. Learning takes place as learners test their mental pictures against experience. As they discover new information that does not fit with their mental pictures, they adapt those pictures by forming new theories or explanations. Teachers can facilitate this process in several ways – by presenting information that challenges their pupils' understandings, for example, or by helping pupils to take guesses in order to formulate new hypotheses.

Because it can take time for learners to reformulate their mental pictures of the world, learning does not necessarily proceed smoothly or continuously. As anyone who has spent much time in the classroom is likely to have noticed, learning sometimes takes place in a series of stops and starts.

How may your schemes of work facilitate cognitivist learning? Well, arguably the very idea of a scheme of work (as opposed to merely a series of one-off lesson plans) is a cognitivist concept – so in designing a scheme of work at all you are probably already on the road to promoting cognitivist learning.

Beyond that, it is important to begin your lesson planning by trying to see the subject through your pupils' eyes and to take as your starting point pupils' knowledge as it is at the moment. 'Start where the pupils are at', as experienced colleagues often put it. Then – and this is the core of cognitivist teaching – concentrate as you present new material on linking it explicitly and coherently with your pupils' existing understanding. The governing metaphor for teaching here is that of providing scaffolding, rather than pouring knowledge into empty receptacles.

GESTALT-IST LEARNING

You know that moment when you realize that what you took to be a drawing of a vase can also be seen as a drawing of two heads in profile facing each other? 'Now I get it!' you say. Learning of this type happens in moments of insight. We use phrases such as 'flash of inspiration' to describe it.

Note that such learning involves seeing a new pattern (or 'Gestalt', as psychologists, drawing on German, say). Typically it involves seeing the whole as more than the sum of the parts – after all, when you come to see the vase drawing as a representation of two faces, the whole has been transformed but the lines (i.e. the parts) have not altered.

Textbooks on education tend to be better at describing Gestalt psychology than explaining how to plan for it. Indeed, learning through Gestalt often seems unpredictable. How could anyone have known that it would be on the road to Damascus that Paul would experience his conversion?

In practice, however, there do seem to be some ways of encouraging such learning. First, you need to remember the importance of wholes. If, for example, you want pupils to learn how deadening clichés can be, you need not simply provide a list of examples of clichés but also show their effect through an entire passage of prose.

Second, simply remembering to describe or explain something more than once – and not in the same way – can often do the trick. A teacher who explains something first in colloquial terms and then in academic language can jolt a pupil into an understanding of the latter. A student who, say, reads a page of economic theory uncomprehendingly might find the same theory immediately clear when it is expressed in the form of a graph.

Third, harness the power of sensual experience. Encouraging learning the Gestalt way involves a lot of gesticulating, pointing, indicating, showing and so on. Sometimes the best way to teach poetic rhythm, for example, is simply to read poetry aloud as well as possible.

Over the years educators have produced a variety of taxonomies for describing the cognitive structure of learning. For the purposes of this book I have decided to divide learning into four broad categories, namely:

1 Knowledge and understanding.
2 Skills, techniques, and methods (Idea 21).
3 Attitudes and perspectives (Idea 22).
4 Judgements and decisions (Idea 23).

Teachers often make a rough and ready distinction between 'knowing that' and 'knowing how'. By 'knowledge' in the above taxonomy I refer to the former.

There are two types of knowledge-in-the-sense-of-knowing-that: (a) empirical knowledge and (b) conceptual knowledge. For example, understanding the distinction between weather and climate is a form of conceptual knowledge, knowing what the average annual rainfall is in Wales is a form of empirical knowledge.

I do not think I have ever seen a scheme of work that fails to specify the knowledge to be acquired (whereas in days gone by I have seen schemes that consisted of nothing *but* a specification of such knowledge!) However, schemes of work do sometimes fail to distinguish between empirical and conceptual knowledge. Whenever this happens there is a danger that the latter gets lost – that in the haste to teach the former, the latter fails to receive explicit attention.

When writing a scheme of work, distinguish between empirical and conceptual knowledge and ensure that you do not neglect the latter.

Knowledge – at least in the sense of knowing-that (see Idea 19) – gets rather a bad press in contemporary education. The educator who insists on the value of this kind of knowledge is likely to be dismissed as a reincarnation of Mr Gradgrind, the deeply unattractive headmaster in Dickens's *Hard Times*. There is a feeling that in these days of increasingly sophisticated search engines we no longer need to store copious amounts of knowledge in our heads – we can use the Internet instead.

We need to reconsider. E.D. Hirsch in his book *Cultural Literacy* refers to an experiment in which some American students were given a passage that referred to Robert E. Lee and Ulysses S. Grant. Many of them failed to understand the passage for the simple reason that they did not know who Lee and Grant were.

Hirsch points out that public discourse is full of references and allusions such as these. Democracy needs citizens with extensive knowledge. Yet often that knowledge need not run very deep – maybe all we need to know about Lee and Grant is that the former fought for the Confederates and the latter for the Unionists in the American Civil War. We can probably get by without knowing what Lee's middle name was.

Hirsch argues that as pupils progress through education we place increasing emphasis on intensive knowledge (knowing a lot about a little) rather than extensive knowledge (knowing a little about a lot). A pupil might, for example, spend a term studying *Romeo and Juliet* yet be unable to name any of Shakespeare's comedies. It's the kind of thing that gets education a bad name.

Look for opportunities to *extend* your pupils' knowledge. Don't dismiss the value of quizzes and research homeworks. Include in your schemes of work an introduction to key reference sources. In doing so you will find that, far from becoming the next Gradgrind, you will be tapping into the fascination with general knowledge that makes TV and pub quizzes so popular.

It was Edward, by the way.

In Idea 19 I proposed a four-fold taxonomy for learning outcomes, one part of which consisted of skills, techniques and methods. 'Skill', 'technique' and 'method' are, of course, far from perfect synonyms – there are important distinctions to be made between them. My reason for lumping them together is simply that they resemble each other far more than they resemble other items in that taxonomy. They bear a family resemblance.

Developing skill has long been a central concern of sports coaching and for that reason I believe that teachers can learn (not only in teaching PE) from the literature of coaching.

That literature suggests that to teach a skill we need first do some analysis. Ask yourself the following questions about the skill or set of skills you wish to teach:

○ What is its purpose?
○ What distinct elements are there?
○ How are they organized into a pattern or sequence?
○ What cues are there to signal when to perform each element of the skill?

Once you have done this, the process of instruction is largely a matter of common sense. Common sense, though, is easily forgotten – so here is a checklist for skills instruction:

○ Check that the instruction you are intending to give is unambiguous and as precise as possible.
○ Skills may be performed at different levels: what level is appropriate for your class?
○ How can you make the instruction process as brief as possible so that the pupils' attention does not wane?
○ Are you in danger of overloading pupils with too much advice at the same time?
○ How can you use expressive language, gesture or humour constructively?

ATTITUDES

As teachers we are often equivocal about attitude. In our schemes of work we might shy away from specifying the teaching of attitudes, thinking it smacks too much of indoctrination. When we come to discuss our pupils, however – whether formally or informally – we often pay a good deal of attention to their attitudes.

We should remember both that attitudes can be taught without being forced on people and that there are plenty of attitudes worth teaching. These fall into two categories. First, there are attitudes (perhaps 'perspectives' would be a happier term) related to particular disciplines. Consider the way that social science requires detachment or at least selectiveness in attention: the sociologist, for example, puts aside the question of whether a particular doctrine is true and asks instead, 'Who holds this belief? What social effects does it have?' The social psychologist studying love affairs points out, rather unromantically, that bonds tend to form between partners who are available, in proximity to each other, and of comparable physical attractiveness.

Second, there are attitudes that cut across subject boundaries – a concern for quality, for example, or a willingness to take responsibility.

In teaching attitudes it may well help to discuss them – to label them, define them, share them, discuss when they are appropriate and why they are valuable – but discussion on its own will only get so far. We also need to exhibit those attitudes ourselves. Pupils are reluctant to do what we say if it isn't also what we do. When incorporating attitudes into our schemes of work, therefore, we need to ask both which attitudes we wish to teach and how we can model them ourselves.

It would be very uncommon for a teacher to forget to specify in their schemes of work the knowledge and skills that they wish their pupils to acquire. We do, however, commonly forget to specify the type of judgements and decisions that they need to learn to make.

It's very easy to assume that, so long as pupils acquire the necessary knowledge and skills, they will automatically be able to make judgements and decisions intelligently. A moment's reflection shows that life isn't like that. Think what it's like to learn to drive, for example – or in sport how differently players perform in an actual match compared to training.

Build tasks into your schemes of work that require your pupils to arrive at judgements and make decisions. Ask them, for example, to rank or rate alternatives, express and justify preferences or draw conclusions. The use of games, role-play and simulations are often particularly effective here – but even very traditional forms such as essays and debates can be (re)designed to emphasize this dimension of learning.

JUDGEMENT AND DECISION-MAKING

THE PLACE OF EMOTIONAL EDUCATION

One pupil I taught was asked in a tutorial to complete a survey about the school. The instructions on how to complete the survey said, 'Please avoid emotion in your comments.' The girl's response to the survey was simply to ring those words and write next to them, 'That's what's wrong with the school.' I mentioned to a colleague that I thought the girl was entirely right – the business of school was to *educate* emotions rather than avoid them. 'But surely,' he said, 'emotions are just things we have? We can't educate them!'

I think he was expressing, very concisely, a commonly held view. I also think he was wrong, for two reasons. First, we typically have emotions *about* something – a situation, person, experience or whatever. This raises the question of the appropriateness of our emotions – fear, relief, remorse, and so on. Has the object of our emotion been clearly and accurately perceived? Is our response the right one? Such questions, concerning perception, efficacy, and ethics, are definitely the stuff of education.

Second, emotion can be articulated – by poets, novelists, and so on. It is commonly thought in expressive arts that emotion precedes the work of art – that the artist first experiences the emotion and then finds words for it. But try looking at the relationship the other way round – it may be that, by articulating an emotion for us, an artwork makes that emotion available to us and enables us to share in it. I think I know how Macbeth feels, even though I haven't murdered many kings myself.

In defining the learning objectives that we intend to achieve, therefore, we should ask ourselves how our schemes of work can contribute to pupils' emotional education.

It is now widely accepted that pupils' preferred learning styles vary. Various taxonomies of learning style exist. The one I have always preferred is derived from the work of David Kolb. It divides learning into four types, that is, learning from:

o theory and generalization;
o the concrete and the particular (see Idea 26);
o reflection (see Idea 27);
o activity – 'learning by doing' (see Idea 28).

Whichever taxonomy you use, beware of one pitfall in particular. Once you think you have identified a pupil's preferred learning style, the temptation is to teach to that style all the time. We should surely be doing the opposite – helping pupils to develop into broader, more adaptable learners. For this reason and because you are likely to have a variety of pupils in your class, aim in your teaching of each topic to include all four of the above learning styles.

When planning to develop theoretical learning, think of 'theory' in two ways:

1 The rigorous scientific meaning, i.e. theory as a set of testable hypotheses, often with one hypothesis deduced from another.
2 The looser, more informal sense, i.e. theory as generalization or overview – the forest without the trees.

To promote (1), try to state the ideas that you wish to study in the form of explicit hypotheses. To promote (1) and (2), ensure that you explore, use and explain the language of theory and generalization: 'therefore', 'typically', 'consequently', and so on. If pupils are going to use such language themselves, they need to hear it from you.

PLANNING FOR THEORETICAL LEARNING

PLANNING FOR LEARNING FROM THE CONCRETE

You can think of learning from the concrete as the opposite of learning from generalization and theory (see Idea 25). In place of generalizations, axioms, probabilistic statements and deductive logic, we have particular instances, examples, case studies.

I confess it took me a long time to appreciate the power of learning from the concrete. I realize now that as a student myself I tended to focus on theory – I would sometimes skip the case studies in textbooks, for example. When I began teaching, therefore, I wasn't alert enough to the way that, for some pupils at least, a topic can suddenly become clear when taught through concrete examples. It probably isn't irrelevant to add that, having come to appreciate this type of learning from a teaching perspective, I am now much keener to learn that way myself.

Seek to include in your teaching of any topic at least a session dedicated to learning from the concrete. Use one or both of the two great staples of concrete learning – the worked example and the case study. Use the latter not only to illustrate prior theoretical points but also as possible starting points for investigating a topic.

There are two ways to draw on reflective learning. The first is by encouraging pupils to reflect on aspects of their life in general – things that they have learnt beforehand, whether in or out of school. The second is by encouraging pupils to reflect on what they have already learnt or experienced within the scheme of work that you are now engaged in.

The first is overlooked by educators to an extraordinary extent. For example, I am at the moment reviewing a textbook about the mass media. Nowhere in the book does the author encourage his readers to reflect on their own experience of the media – yet if there's one thing our pupils are likely to have experience of . . . !

Similarly, last year I wrote a study of the way that literary studies textbooks taught readers about narrative. Almost without exception there was no attempt to encourage readers to relate the discussion to their own experience of narrative, even though most of us have been listening to stories since we were tots.

We need to design opportunities for pupils to reflect explicitly on what they are learning, to relate it to their prior experience and to draw on that experience. To fail to do so is to waste an opportunity to develop their comprehension.

PLANNING FOR REFLECTIVE LEARNING

You can think of active learning as the opposite of reflective learning (see Idea 27). Put crudely, reflective learning involves sitting down and thinking back, whereas active learning involves getting up and doing something new.

Active learning can feature in your planning in two places. Sometimes you can arrange for active learning within your lessons – drama, role-play, observation, conducting surveys, filming, and so on. Sometimes you can build it into the homeworks that you set, such as interviewing, researching and mini fieldwork projects.

Sometimes there are constraints – safety issues, for example, or lack of resources – that prevent you from setting the kind of active learning you'd like to do. If all else fails you can always fall back on hypothetical active learning using conditional verbs in the assignments you set: 'What *would* you do . . . ?', 'How *would* you . . . ?'

The two **BIG** ideas – progression and differentiation

IDEA

29

PLANNING PROGRESSION
FROM PRIOR LEARNING

In planning schemes of work it is important to consider what pupils have learnt before. This helps to ensure both that you make use of such learning and that you move pupils forward.

The links between prior knowledge and the knowledge to be learnt next are not always immediately obvious. In order to identify such links it is helpful to scrutinize the curriculum under the following headings.

1   General learning strategies – techniques, habits of mind, and so on, not related to specific subjects or topics.

2   Contiguous knowledge – knowledge closely associated with that you are planning to teach. For a pupil learning about a certain theme in a certain period of history, examples would include knowledge of other themes in that period.

3   Comparable knowledge – knowledge of a different topic that is sufficiently similar for analogies to be drawn. For example, in technology a pupil might learn about the qualities of one material by comparing it to other materials.

4   'Top-down' knowledge – pupils who have learnt about a general concept (e.g. deforestation) proceed to learn about particular instances (e.g. Amazonia).

5   'Bottom-up' knowledge – pupils who have learnt about particular cases proceed to learn about the general concepts, issues or themes that they exemplify.

6   Other knowledge bearing no necessary relation to the new knowledge to be learnt.

In order to facilitate pupil progression it is helpful to consider in your planning not only what your pupils have learnt in the past but also what they will learn in future terms or years. Schools often miss opportunities by failing to coordinate schemes of work sufficiently between curriculum years.

For example, if pupils are going to be required at one stage of the curriculum to make a thematic study of a novel, you can plan backwards by, say, teaching them to make a thematic study of shorter text – perhaps a short story – at an earlier stage in the curriculum.

You can use the six categories of knowledge outlined in Idea 29 to plan backwards as well as forwards.

PLANNING FUTURE PROGRESSION

CROSS-CURRICULAR LINKS

Schools tend to put learning into boxes with labels such as 'Mathematics, 'Science', and so on. This is problematic because, first, the world that we are preparing pupils to deal with does not come neatly packaged in the same way and, second, because there is a danger that important aspects of the curriculum will disappear down the cracks between subjects. How, for example, does the school ensure that its pupils achieve multicultural awareness?

The problem is compounded by the fact that the most obvious ways of building bridges across the curriculum are not necessarily the most important. Though it does no harm for the teacher of language arts to point out when teaching rhythm that pupils have also studied the topic in music (and perhaps even arrange for the topic to be taught in both subjects at the same time of year), it doesn't necessarily do much good either. Sometimes well-intentioned observations along the lines of, 'You've studied this in music' merely elicit the response, 'So what?' Curriculum mapping can feel disheartening as a result.

I suspect that cross-curricular teaching tends to work more effectively when it is organized around skill (see Idea 21) rather than content. I remember, for example, discovering in a chance conversation with a colleague who taught history that the kind of close-reading of literary texts required by the English syllabus I was teaching resembled that required for study of documents in the history syllabus. When we started to share, compare, and coordinate our efforts there was a clear sense in the classroom that this made sense to the pupils too. It was the first time I felt that my efforts at cross-curricular coordination bore much fruit. On the basis of such experience (rather than on any objective research findings), I recommend focusing cross-curricular planning on the teaching of skill rather than just content.

Differentiation is the process of adapting educational activity to suit the diverse needs and characteristics of the learners. Differentiation is usually divided into three types:

1 By task. You modify the task to suit different students or you set different tasks.
2 By outcome. Pupils attempt the same task (e.g. writing a story) but perform it at different levels or to differing degrees of completion. (I prefer to think in terms of 'expectation' rather than outcome – there are many reasons why learning outcomes vary between pupils, and in practice one has to make a judgement about which variations are acceptable.)
3 By support. You support various pupils – directly, through your own intervention, or indirectly through support from ancillary staff or additional resources.

Learning not to rely on (2) is one of the major leaps in a teacher's development. The first step is to recognize that (a) differentiation is central to effective teaching and (b) it involves careful preparation. Some things in teaching, thank goodness, you can wing – but differentiation isn't one of them.

Say 'differentiation' to a group of colleagues and the chances are that someone will start talking about 'ability'. 'Ability' (which in any case is an ambiguous, poorly defined term) is not the only ground for differentiation. Consider also such criteria as learning style, special educational needs, individual needs (see Idea 33) and bilingualism. Note, in particular, that 'setting by ability' (so-called) does not remove the need for differentiation.

Jim Cummins's ideas, outlined in Idea 34, provide a useful framework for planning differentiation by task.

DIFFERENTIATION

When formulating your plan, you need to consider the assessment data that you already possess for the pupils you are going to teach. I use 'assessment data' in the broadest sense, to include all records concerning pupils' learning. This is likely to include both quantitative and qualitative data. Examples of such data include:

1 Information on the general level at which pupils are working in your subject.
2 Information about bilingualism.
3 Special Needs (upper case S, upper case N): information about pupils regarding conditions such as dyslexia, dyspraxia, emotional and behavioural difficulties, autism, ADHD, language and communication difficulties, physical disability and medical conditions.
4 Individual needs (what I call 'lower-case special needs', in that individual needs are special for the individual concerned). This may include low-level and informal issues, including observations from recent marking, for example, 'Wayne needs to check his paragraphing before handing in his work.'

The purpose of consulting such data while planning is to:

o ensure that you are pitching the lesson in general at the right level;
o consider how to differentiate the lesson (see Idea 32);
o decide what sort of support to offer.

Most people accept the idea of teaching cognitively simple material before the cognitively difficult. For example, we would all teach addition before multiplication. One educator – Jim Cummins – has argued that we need to learn to think equally on a second dimension, namely that of measuring the degree of contextualization. For instance, in teaching spatial patterns we can look at contextualized examples (how children are distributed in the playground at breaktime, for example) or decontextualized ones (e.g. abstract models such as Walter Christaller's Central Place Theory). Putting these two dimensions together yields the following model:

Quadrant B Learning is: 1 Strongly contextualized 2 High in cognitive demand	Quadrant C Learning is: 1 Weakly contextualized 2 High in cognitive demand
Quadrant A Learning is: 1 Strongly contextualized 2 Low in cognitive demand	Quadrant D Learning is: 1 Weakly contextualized 2 Low in cognitive demand

Cummins argues that the ideal path for structuring courses is to start in Quadrant A and then move pupils via Quadrant B to Quadrant C. Teachers need to learn to increase the level of cognitive demand first and then reduce the degree of contextualization. Cummins sees activities in Quadrant D as valueless. The provision of tasks for Quadrant B is often key to pupils' development.

Though Cummins's theory was specifically developed for teaching bilingual pupils, it seems to me very useful when teaching monolingual pupils too. Teachers often adopt a Cummins-ian approach without knowing it. Despite its ungainly jargon, Cummins has proved one of the useful theories I have worked with as a teacher. The framework assists thinking about progression, differentiation (see Idea 32) and assessment – and, above all, planning. Explore it, try it.

For an introductory discussion of Cummins, see Cline & Frederickson, *Curriculum Related Assessment, Cummins and Bilingual Children.*

EXTENSION MATERIAL

The easiest kind of extension material to provide for talented pupils is more of the same: 'You've finished one task, now do another one just like it!' This can be useful for providing practice (see Idea 56) and consolidation. Too often, though, it results in dull repetition and the loss of opportunity to learn more. It's important not to mistake quantity for quality.

The following are useful options for extension tasks:

- a comparable task to the one that the pupil has just done, but more challenging;
- a task that requires the pupil to *transfer* the knowledge they have just acquired to another area or situation;
- a task that requires the pupil to *apply* knowledge they have acquired to a problem.

One useful framework for planning extension tasks is that provided by Jim Cummins's thinking on education. As you'll see from the outline in Idea 34, this highlights two possibilities – increasing the cognitive demand that tasks make on the pupil or making tasks less contextualized.

The role of language

THE IMPORTANCE OF LANGUAGE

Regardless of the subject you are teaching – science, mathematics, dance, whatever – a good deal of your pupils' learning will be acquired through the medium of language. And in most subjects at least part of their assessment outcomes too will be expressed in that medium. Clearly, then, the effectiveness of learning in your classroom is determined in part by the role of language.

Language is such a pervasive part of our environment that there is a danger that we take it for granted. Most teachers do of course recognize that they need to teach their pupils the specialist terminology of their subjects. Teachers of mathematics or geography, for example, teach the meaning of 'parallelogram' and 'glaciation' respectively. But who teaches how to use words such as 'although' or 'therefore' – or to skim-read a document, say, or write a report?

The fundamental point is not to treat language as transparent, but rather to remember that it needs to be taught – and hence to be part of your planning, whatever subject you teach.

As explained in Idea 36, it is important not to think of language as a transparent learning medium – we need to build the use and development of language into our planning.

This certainly applies to listening. Listening activities are often planned carefully in the teaching of foreign languages and music. Elsewhere in the curriculum, listening tends to be thought of only in terms of classroom management.

There are three ways to encourage and develop listening as a means of learning. First, provide opportunities for pupils to listen to a range of voices, not just yours. Make use of teaching assistants, pupils and recorded material. (Many of the most characterful and famous voices of our age, after all, are available on the Internet.) Many teachers take care – through mounting displays and so on – to make their classrooms visually lively, yet sometimes their rooms are aurally sterile.

Second, before presenting information, give pupils focused and selective listening tasks – ask them to identify certain types of information, to see how many examples of some idea they can identify, to sort and record information into boxes, to respond to pre-arranged cues, and so on.

Third, set aural comprehension tests. The best procedure is usually to read, play or perform a piece of material, next present a set of questions, then re-present the material.

IDEA

38

There are many reasons why we need to ensure that we build oral work into our planning. In particular:

1 Speaking helps pupils to learn in a number of ways. It helps them to formulate ideas, for example, and to connect ideas with their own knowledge and experience.
2 It enables pupils to contribute new ideas.
3 By increasing the repertoire of voices that pupils listen to, oral work provides a more varied aural environment (see Idea 37).
4 By encouraging pupils to put their thinking into words, oral work is a useful preparation for writing activities.
5 In some subjects, pupils may fulfil assessment objectives directly through oral work.

Oral work can also help to change the rhythm and complexion of lessons and make learning feel less passive. In planning learning activities, therefore, it is important to seek to balance receptive work – listening, watching, reading – with oral work.

It is, however, worth being aware of one pitfall straightaway. The easiest way to build oral work into one's plans is to include a class discussion. But research shows over and over again that 'class discussion' – in the sense of a dialogue between teacher and class – is (especially in terms of speaking time) heavily dominated by the teacher. The total number of minutes' speech contributed by pupils to such discussions tends to be small and the average amount of speech per pupil negligible. Ideas 39 and 40 provide alternatives to this scenario.

Pair discussion is less public – and for that reason usually less intimidating – than other kinds of discussion. Pair work usually requires little or no reorganisation of furniture and so can be set up quickly. It can be useful, therefore, as a way of changing the rhythm of a lesson or building momentum. It can be particularly useful for activities such as:

o generating a list of questions;
o preparing a statement about some issue or a definition of some concept;
o revising a task or piece of work;
o planning a method to adopt for a task;
o reviewing and clarifying a text or other learning resource.

Pair work can also be very useful as a preparation for other, larger scale discussions. The opportunity to discuss an issue in pairs before a class discussion, for example, can help to give pupils confidence. Often the least fussy, most direct way to set up a small group discussion is simply to ask one pair to turn its chairs round and join another pair to compare their results on a task that they have both just completed.

Consider, therefore, building pair work into your planning both as a valuable learning activity in its own right and as a preparation for other activities.

THE PLACE OF PAIR WORK

SMALL GROUP DISCUSSION

Small group discussion can be fantastically rewarding. It offers a great way of involving pupils, generating ideas and finding out what pupils think and have understood. On the other hand, it can be dire – pupils fail to engage with the task, run out of steam, talk irrelevantly, distract each other, become noisy and disorderly, etc.

It is best to establish conventions by using small group discussion little and often to begin with. Allow time to talk explicitly about conventions – who sits where, who fulfils which roles (chair, scribe, spokesperson, etc.)

When small group discussion fails to meet expectations, it is often because of inadequate planning. When planning small group discussion, consider:

○ whether you are giving pupils enough opportunity to prepare through individual or pair work;
○ whether the task is sufficiently engaging;
○ how you can ensure that pupils understand the material that they are supposed to discuss;
○ what outcomes you are going to specify;
○ how you are going to indicate the depth of discussion required;
○ how much time to allow (note in particular that, if you allow too much time, the pace will slacken or pupils will finish early);
○ whether you have sufficiently analysed the task or whether it needs to be broken down more (see Idea 50).

The point of this list is by no means to discourage you from including small group discussion in your lesson plans: it is simply to emphasize the need for planning and to show what type is required.

Whole class discussion has an obvious educational value. It enables questions to be raised and viewpoints to be expressed and tested. It gives pupils experience of talking in front of an audience, and teachers an opportunity to assess the class's understanding of a subject. But it doesn't always work very well.

That such discussion isn't always successful is hardly surprising. The demands that it makes on participants are much greater than those of an ordinary conversation. You can maximize the chances of success by planning carefully.

The key is to give pupils a chance to prepare. The following provide opportunities for this:

o dedicating the homework that precedes the lesson to preparatory activities such as doing research or writing a position statement;
o setting an agenda;
o setting pair work in advance;
o setting small group work in advance.

It often helps to do more than one type of preparatory activity before the discussion.

One way to organize the discussion is to use the following three-phase structure:

1 Elicit statements about personal experience, standpoints or research.
2 Then widen the discussion by (a) deepening the discussion (usually with how or why questions) and/or (b) introducing fresh material or a new, provocative perspective.
3 Provide a definite sense of conclusion by, for example, asking pupils to help summarize the discussion into a specified number of points or reach a decision.

The best book on the subject – in fact, one of the best books I've read on teaching of any kind – is the little-known *Expanding Horizons* by Alan Howe. As soon as I started to follow the advice given in that book, the whole class discussions in my lessons improved. Get it, read it, do it!

PLANNING READING

Once I was involved in a whole school survey to see what pupils actually did in lessons. It revealed that one thing pupils did very little of – to my mind, frighteningly little – was reading. In that, our school was far from unique.

An even worse picture emerges when one looks in detail at the way reading is used across the curriculum. In many lessons in many schools pupils do virtually no sustained reading: reading is limited to very short texts (worksheets, web pages – or fragments thereof). What is more, the pupils' reading is often done for them. The teacher displays a PowerPoint slide or distributes a handout and then immediately reads it all through aloud. The message this sends is that pupils do not need to read – that reading is not how one learns.

As a corrective, consider the fact that pupils' reading ability is closely interrelated to the amount of reading they do (measured in number of words). Good readers become so largely by reading a lot. Starving weak readers of text virtually guarantees slow development.

It is useful to audit your schemes of work by asking:

○ How much reading are you expecting of pupils?
○ How much opportunity are you providing for sustained reading?
○ How often do you not read a text out (at least not straightaway)?
○ How far do you challenge pupils to learn from texts before you intervene?
○ How often do you *just let pupils read* (without feeling that there has to be e.g. a test, a written outcome, a discussion)?

The following technique – adapted from the long-forgotten Kingman Report (Idea 48) – can be used to teach pupils how to understand a variety of texts – not only written texts but also video or audio material.

Select a text that you want your pupils to understand. Prepare a plan to work through it in the following four stages.

1   For each sentence or segment of the text, clarify what is called the 'thin' meaning (the type of meaning it might have if it were taken *out* of context). Concentrate on helping pupils to recognize words and to see how they fit into meaningful sequences (sometimes just reading aloud will do this).
2   Then clarify what each phrase *refers* to (e.g. what does it represent or indicate?).
3   Then ask what the writer (or speaker) is presupposing. What, for example, does s/he assume the reader knows or believes?
4   Finally, clarify what is called the 'thick' meaning. For example, why is the writer (or speaker) saying this? What point is s/he making? What effect is s/he trying to achieve?

In my experience, (3) is the most difficult to teach – even when you use relatively simple phrases (such as 'assume' or 'take for granted') to convey the idea of presupposition. But (3) is, I suggest, extraordinarily important in helping pupils to deal with challenging texts at whatever level they are working at.

Note that the technique can be used with texts of varying lengths, including very short ones.

IDEA

44

When pupils use books to learn from, we tend to locate and select information for them, for example, 'Turn to page 58'. It is important at some point, however, to show them how to use whole books.

Set a quiz based on a book. Ensure that each answer requires the pupil to use some sort of information-handling device. Examples of such devices include:

o Contents page.
o Section numbering.
o Page numbering.
o Sub-headings.
o Figures.
o Tables and charts.
o Bold or italicized print.
o Cross-references.
o Footnotes or endnotes.
o Bibliography.
o Glossary.
o Index.

Ideally you need a set of books of some description. I was once fortunate enough to be given a class set of a well-known travel guide to Australia. I could set questions such as, 'Recommend a hotel near the main railway station in Brisbane.' Pupils needed to think, 'Where is information about Brisbane? Is there a section on accommodation? Is there a map?' and so on. Strangely, the question that they always found most difficult to answer was, 'Name three building materials used in Australia and give examples of famous buildings using these materials.' Much scanning, skimming and scratching of heads followed. Hardly anybody thought to look at the colour photographs and their captions.

I mentioned in Idea 42 a survey, conducted in one school that I taught in, of the allocation of pupils' time in lessons. While pupils spent very little time reading, they spent a huge amount of time writing. Again, I do not think the school was unique in this. If learning correlated at all strongly with the amount of time spent writing, our schools would be turning out hundreds of thousands of geniuses! That they're not suggests that there is something amiss with the way we use writing in teaching.

This idea is a plea to focus on the quality of pupils' writing as opposed to the quantity. The biggest single step a teacher can make in developing their pupils' writing is to understand that writing is not just a product, but also a process. Much of the writing that pupils do in school is done straight off, in one sitting.

To see how unconducive that approach is to quality, consider the ways in which you yourself write. There may be certain types of writing that you approach in that way, either because it's trivial (e.g. an email dashed off to a friend) or because you're expert at it. But the chances are that you don't approach all or even most writing tasks like that. What, for example, do you do when you are writing a job application? The likelihood is that you adopt a process approach in which you revisit the text that you are producing.

The simplest process model comprises two stages: (1) drafting; (2) checking. Even just adopting that approach – and teaching pupils *how* to check (see Idea 71) – would, I suggest, improve the quality of much of our pupils' writing. For a more sophisticated approach to written work, give thought to the following five stages of the writing process: (1) planning and preparation; (2) drafting; (3) redrafting; (4) checking; and (5) presenting. You may not wish to include all five of these stages in each and every writing assignment, but the above list at least provides a menu from which you can select.

People tend to find writing easier when they've seen some examples of the kind of thing – CV, grant application, business letter or whatever – that they are supposed to be producing. In schools, however, we sometimes do expect pupils to write in forms for which we have not provided models. (When I was a pupil I had to write a lot of essays. I would have found it much easier if at some point someone had shown me what essays look like!)

Before setting a written task, prepare some models for pupils to study. If, for instance, you want pupils to write reports, show them some examples of reports. There are two types of model:

o those written by experts – often professionally written and published;
o those written by other pupils.

Both have their uses. The former have the virtue, obviously, of displaying expertise, but for that same reason can be daunting – they can seem too remote from pupils' own attempts. Models provided by other pupils are less expert, but more approachable and often more imitable.

When using the latter, I suggest that you use examples of work from a comparable but different assignment, rather than previous attempts at the same task. That way, pupils can gain ideas about tone, style, structure, etc. without either plagiarising or slavishly imitating.

Imagine you had to write an account of your school. Wouldn't you want to know whom it was for? Wouldn't the way you wrote it vary according to whether it was for, say, other colleagues, a prospectus, a researcher or a magazine editor? It is the same for our pupils.

There are two main types of writing: that written for impersonal, unspecified, audiences (essays typically fall into this category) and that written for specified audiences, that is, for particular, known readers (letters, for example). Pupils need to learn how to write both. Often, however, they find the latter easier. The specification of audience helps them to make decisions about tone, vocabulary, etc. One of the best pieces of coursework I have ever received was from a pupil who, when writing about her favourite novel, decided to produce a letter to me instead of an essay. 'Dear Mr Haynes': those three words made all the difference for her.

Audit the written tasks you set and ask yourself whether those aimed at impersonal audiences can be converted into pieces for (either actual or hypothetical) personal ones.

TEACHING ABOUT SUBJECT DISCOURSE

Sir John Kingman FRS is still alive. That means that there are at least two people on this planet who remember the report resulting from the committee that he chaired – the *Report of the Committee of Inquiry into the Teaching of English Language* (1988). Kenneth Baker, the Minister who commissioned the report, greeted it as 'interesting'(by which he meant 'very disappointing') and consigned it to the dustbin.

Though the report was roundly criticized, it contained some ideas that I have used with success in the classroom. One such idea concerns the teaching of the structure of language. The Kingman Report recommended that pupils should be taught not only the structure of sentences (i.e. grammar) but also discourse structure, that is, the way that texts are structured beyond the level of the sentence.

Take, for example, a page from, say, a textbook or website in your subject. Number the sentences. Study the way the passage moves from one sentence to another. Support your teaching by preparing a set of questions for your pupils based on the following types:

o What does each new sentence add (new information, more information about the same point, an opinion, or what)?
o What is the purpose of each new sentence?
o How does the new sentence relate to the previous one – does it, for example, repeat, amplify, develop, qualify or negate it?

You can do the same by looking at paragraphs rather than sentences.

Building such study into your lessons will help pupils both to understand material that they read in your subject and to structure their own written work. And you needn't worry that you are duplicating the work of your pupils' English (or language arts) teachers: they'll have long forgotten Sir John, even if they had ever heard of him.

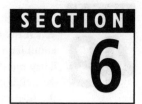

Pedagogy

CLASSROOM LAYOUT

One evening I was preparing to teach a class of adults. When the first couple of students arrived I asked if they could lend a hand moving some of the tables and chairs. They burst out laughing. When I asked them why, they said, 'It's just that we've noticed that however you find the furniture, you *always* reorganize it!'

This was true. Arranging furniture is one of the most powerful and direct means for designing, and influencing the style of, lessons. A few years later I met a social psychologist called Nigel Hastings, who confirmed this view. He had researched children's learning in classrooms and found that seating patterns made a discernible impact.

Clearly, then, it is worth giving some thought to which patterns suit different kinds of lessons – and experiment with different layouts. It may help to consider one of Hastings's main findings. He found that in many primary classrooms pupils sit in small groups around tables. His research had found that for many of the kinds of learning that the pupils were actually required to do – individual work, for example, or whole class discussion – this arrangement made learning harder and teaching less effective.

Task analysis is the cornerstone of lesson planning. One of the reasons that lessons fail is that we try to teach complex material without providing pupils with sufficient preparation.

Take the main task that you wish to teach. Analyse it to see how it can be broken down into a series of smaller 'bite-sized' chunks or sub-tasks. The lesson can then proceed through a series of simple steps, starting with something that pupils already know and ending with the most complex part of the task. This procedure has sometimes been described metaphorically as starting with a molecule, analysing it into the constituent atoms, presenting each atom to the pupils, and finally showing how the atoms are arranged to form the molecule.

Though task analysis sounds unexciting and perhaps rather obvious, it is all too easy to do it sloppily. There are a various criteria you can use to ensure that you have analysed a task rigorously:

1 Have you analysed all aspects of the task?
2 Have you reduced the main task too far? Too many very small sub-tasks lead to confusion: the pupils will not be able to see the wood for the trees.
3 Is it clear to everyone where one sub-task ends and another begins?
4 Are you clear about the level of skill with which you expect each sub-task to be performed?

Let's borrow an idea from higher education. In *53 Interesting things to do in your seminars and tutorials*, Graham Gibbs argues that it is important at the start of a teaching session to 'orientate' students. He points out that often when they enter the room they have come from various places and activities (with, it should be added, all kinds of things occupying their minds). A process of orientation will help to gain their attention.

Gibbs recommends three simple stages:

1 Arrange the room to suit the class you are going to teach (see Idea 49).
2 Greet students as they arrive. Chat to the early-birds about your course while the others come in.
3 Then start the session proper by relating it straightaway to the previous one and to the course as a whole.

I suggest that this process is useful in school too, especially in secondary education.

In his book *The Psychology of Teaching and Learning*, educational psychologist Manuel Martinez-Pons argues that successful teachers (a) have a clear idea of what they have wanted their pupils to be able to do and (b) have used a certain general structure for their lessons.

In outline, the recommended structure consists of the following stages:

1 Introduction.
2 Exposition.
3 Clarification.
4 Enactment.
5 Feedback.
6 Transfer.
7 Deliberate practice.

In (1) the teacher explains the objectives of the lesson and seeks to motivate the pupils. In (2) the pedagogical methods vary. Success, Martinez-Pons suggests, depends most on the level of the teacher's expertise in (a) the subject matter and (b) subject-specific pedagogy. In (3) the pupils and teacher check and sharpen understanding by asking each other questions. In (4) the pupils do whatever it is the teacher has just taught them to do. In (5) the teacher not only provides hints, suggestions, and corrections, but also encourages the pupils to reflect on their learning. In (6) the teacher helps pupils to move beyond the immediate task and think of ways to apply their learning more widely. In (7) pupils continue to rehearse what they have just learnt.

A SUCCESSFUL LESSON STRUCTURE

AN ALTERNATIVE WAY TO STRUCTURE LESSONS

In his book *Teaching as Story Telling*, Kieran Egan argues against many of the approaches – setting objectives, moving from the simple to the complex, etc. – used in books such as the one you are reading. He believes that such approaches ignore the power of children's imagination. As an alternative, he advocates structuring lessons to resemble stories.

Egan notes that many stories are structured around binary opposites, that is, pairs of ideas or forces that are in some sense set against each other. The story ends only when this struggle is resolved or completed in some way.

Egan's method for lesson planning proceeds along the following lines:

1 Analyse the topic that you wish to teach. Ask yourself: what is important about it? Which aspects of it should matter to your pupils? What will they find most engaging?
2 Find a pair of binary opposites that best capture these aspects of the topic.
3 For your lesson content, use materials that most strikingly display the relationship between these binary opposites. You can then structure the 'story' that your lesson tells around these materials.

Egan emphasizes this approach is not only for language- or arts-based subjects such as English or drama. In fact, large swathes of the curriculum lend themselves quite naturally to organization around binary opposites. Think, for example, of the potential of the following pairings: continuity and change; structure and process; order and chaos; appearance and reality; general and particular; public and private; individual and community.

First, there is the obvious way: state – and explain – the aim and objectives of the lesson.

Second, there is the problem-centred approach. Outline a problem in your subject (e.g. why does gas tend to expand as it is heated?) Draw as much attention to problematic aspects as possible. Then explain that the main part of the lesson will be devoted to investigating and solving the problem. A variation is to state a hypothesis to be tested.

Third, there is what has become known as the 'advance organizer'. At the start of the lesson you present a statement that might strike pupils as problematic, unclear, confusing or mistaken. You then use the lesson to provide the context and knowledge necessary to understand the statement. At the end of the lesson, you return to the statement – preferably to gasps of enlightenment!

Fourth, begin straightaway with a written test. This is helpful when you start teaching a topic in order to ascertain what pupils already know. It also sends a useful 'No messing' signal.

PACE – AND RHYTHM

Talk to people who regularly observe lessons and they will tell you that pace is very important. Good lessons tend to feel pacy. Slow lessons tend to produce poor results – and to unravel as everyone gets bored. And, of course, as they unravel, progress becomes even slower. To set a good pace it helps not only to plan the lesson schedule accurately but also to regard your estimates as a challenge – can you and the class get through the material sooner than that?

One sometimes hears people talk about pace in teaching as if it's *always* a case of the more pace, the better. But that is a simplification. Sometimes you need to relax the pace. This is where it helps to consider an oft-ignored concept, namely rhythm. Though some activities, such as question-and-answer sessions, usually benefit from a brisk pace, others – many types of reading, for example, or the planning of a project – sometimes require patience.

It is often helpful to vary the rhythm by building in different types of activity. This is particularly important where lessons are long – a frantic pace eventually becomes wearing for the teacher and taxing for the pupils. Certainly it is important if you are timetabled for a double lesson to think of it as a session requiring its own rhythm, different from that of a single lesson. In particular, it helps to build in milestones that provide, for both you and your pupils, a clear sense of progress and achievement within the lesson.

In Idea 52 'deliberate practice' was listed as one of the components of a general structure for successful lessons. Thought needs to be given, however, to the nature of practice to be given. It is all too easy to write 'practice' in your lesson plan without considering what type of practice is most appropriate.

There are four main types of practice:

1 Drills.
2 Variable practice.
3 Massed practice.
4 Distributed practice.

(1) consists of a set routine of well-defined, closed, discrete skills. It is useful for maintaining skills already learnt and for developing efficiency, so that the skills become 'second nature'.

(2) is useful for less defined, more open skills. It involves both repetition and variation. For example, a football player can practise the skill of shooting at goal, but from various positions. Variable practice helps to maintain interest and motivation.

(3) involves sessions of continuous practice, with no break within sessions. Massed practice is best used to develop simple skills in short sessions.

(4) involves breaks and rests between practice attempts. These can allow time for reflection and mental rehearsal. Distributed practice is useful for developing difficult, complex skills. It is particularly suitable for learners with low motivation or short attention spans.

Planning, then, involves thinking not only about when to provide practice, but also how.

When planning an instructional lesson, you may find the following structure – outlined in *Lesson Planning and Class Management* by K. Paul Kasambira – helpful. On page 23 of that book, Kasambira suggests three stages:

1 Introduction.
2 Presentation.
3 Conclusion.

The main purpose of (1) is to gain the pupils' attention and whet their appetites.

For (2), it is obviously important to organize material clearly. Kasambira suggests selecting from the following three patterns for organization:

○ Chronological sequence: a step-by-step approach, typically moving from the earliest stage of a process to the latest. (This approach is often compatible with the use of narrative.)
○ Categorical order: for example, outlining arguments first for, and then against, a position. (Another example would be moving through successive stages of a hierarchy.)
○ Problem-solution model: first define and analyse a problem, then provide or explore solutions.

Stage (3) has three main purposes:

○ to summarize the main points that have been learnt;
○ to summarize how learning from the lesson may be applied;
○ to provide precise guidance on follow-up activities.

We all know that there are problems with chalk-and-talk as a teaching method. Pupils don't listen (even if they look attentive); or they listen for a while but then their attention strays; or they listen but don't understand; or they understand but promptly forget it all.

Nevertheless, it remains a common method and isn't going to disappear. The key point is that, if we're going to chalk-and-talk, we might as well do it well. For all the difficulties involved, good chalk-and-talk is better than bad.

Some of the factors behind good chalk-and-talk are matters of performance rather than planning – matters such as speaking audibly, using expressive body language, making eye contact, and so on. But others are very much the product of planning.

Here, then, is a list of factors that benefit chalk-and-talk sessions.

1   Mastery of the subject matter.
2   The age-old technique of (a) telling 'em what you're going to say, (b) telling it, (c) telling 'em what you've told 'em.
3   Starting with something enigmatic, paradoxical, counterintuitive or dramatic.
4   An easily understood, clearly discernible structure, such as chronological sequence, acrostics, problem-and-solution, thesis-antithesis-synthesis, extended analogy, hierarchy (e.g. bronze, silver, gold).
5   Including both generalization/principle/theory and concrete examples.
6   Drawing on pupils' own experience.
7   Enlivening your speech with metaphor.
8   Telling (relevant) jokes.
9   Mixing first, second and third person discourse.
10 Repetition of key phrases (motifs).
11 Using catch phrases, soundbites, slogans, mottoes, mnemonics.

PREPARATION FOR CHALK-AND-TALK

DEATH BY POWERPOINT

When I first came across PowerPoint, I thought, 'What a fantastic tool'. I have been growing less enchanted ever since. It has some undoubted uses. It's great for presenting visual material (e.g. pie charts), for displaying quotations and references, and for reinforcing key terms (especially with second-language learners). But there are also problems with using PowerPoint.

When preparing a PowerPoint presentation, use the following checklist to help avoid the most common pitfalls:

○ Are any of the slides too cramped? Can I reduce the amount of information on each slide?
○ When do I need to ask the class to focus on the screen?
○ When do I want them to focus on me as speaker? How can I use body language or audience interaction to encourage this?
○ How can I vary my speaking position in order to establish eye contact and rapport?
○ When should I turn off the display?

The important point is to ensure that you use PowerPoint for the benefit of the class, rather than simply as an *aide-mémoire* for you. Use PowerPoint – but do so sparingly, selectively, intelligently.

I once heard a guest speaker lecture on the rise of the Ottoman Empire. He explained the various reasons why the empire had grown, adding at one point that, 'Of course, the spread of the empire was helped by the growth of railways.'

A few minutes later he said, 'I said that the growth of the empire was helped by the growth of railways, but of course this isn't true. There weren't any railways in those days, they hadn't been invented. I just said it to see if any of you were listening.'

The reason this technique is a useful one to have in your quiver is that it wakes up not only those people who aren't listening, but also those who are listening but not thinking. It prompts the listener to think, 'How did I miss that?' When you're planning a session of chalk-and-talk, prepare whatever is the equivalent of Ottoman railways for your subject.

RAILWAYS AND THE OTTOMAN EMPIRE

MODELLING

Don't worry, this doesn't involve catwalks. One of the ways we learn is by modelling ourselves on other people. We watch, say, an expert golfer and then try to imitate him or her. If you reflect on the informal learning you've done in your life – learning how to do housework, for example – you might well find that modelling has played a role in much of it.

Modelling is an under-used technique in school. Teachers can be reluctant to say, 'Do it the way I do!' – perhaps they feel that is too prescriptive, perhaps they are too modest. It is frustrating, however, to think that teachers who are expert in various things sometimes fail to provide opportunities for pupils to learn by modelling. Imagine watching a cookery programme in which the celebrity chef refrains from cooking!

Imagine, for example, you want to teach children to appreciate a piece of poetry. There are various ways of approaching the problem. You can, for example, start with the pupils' own responses. Or you can ask questions designed to direct their attention to certain features. But another way is to show how you yourself approach the task. Work through the poem by thinking aloud. Show what problems you encounter, what questions you pose, what strategies you employ. Show how your understanding develops.

Some of the best examples I've seen of this, incidentally, are when teachers have put classes together for a revision session. The teachers have formed a panel and given each other questions or exercises to think through in public.

Think of yourself, if not as Naomi Campbell, then as the Jamie Oliver of your subject.

When I was a pupil, I learnt that there were certain teachers with a propensity for going off at a tangent. That is, a well-placed question from a pupil would be likely to distract the teacher from whatever boring topic they were teaching into some lengthy, irrelevant discourse on something else altogether. At most of the schools where I've taught there has been at least one teacher with such a reputation.

The interesting point about red herrings is that pupils seem to enjoy them, tell you about them, and remember them. The fact that pupils remember them makes me suspect that the colleagues responsible are not so naïve as their pupils think. Is launching into a red herring a way of teaching pupils about a topic that, if it were announced as the main subject of the lesson, they would affect to find boring? I suggest you indulge yourself occasionally.

THE RED HERRING

QUESTION TIME

While preparing to write this book I consulted a number of sources about effective teaching. I was interested to note that the majority view was that good lessons include questioning. What's more, most people who hold that view also believe that some of the questions should be raised by the pupils.

There are several good reasons for teachers to ask questions of pupils. Doing so helps teachers to assess what has been understood, for example, and also to extend or deepen pupils' learning. Encouraging pupils to pose questions helps them to articulate thought, express difficulties, check their understanding, acquire more information and explore possibilities. All of which makes questioning a good use of time.

But note that word 'encouraging'. Questioning doesn't just happen – in fact it is quite easy inadvertently to prevent a questioning ethos from arising. Questioning is encouraged by a heuristic pedagogy on your part. If, for example, you begin lessons by posing problems and then explore possible solutions, that is likely to encourage a questioning mentality. If your own questioning is open and genuine (as opposed to closed, rhetorical questioning, which is sadly still common), that too will help. You can make it a routine that pupils have to think of some questions before answering the one you've set. And some of your assignments can require students to frame some questions instead of writing answers.

I vividly recall observing a colleague teach a lesson on Shakespeare. The subject of the lesson was a scene from *A Midsummer Night's Dream*. He asked the pupils a series of questions. He never said that the answers were wrong (in fact, he frequently said, 'Right' or 'OK') but he didn't seem altogether satisfied. Interestingly, the questions became more directive ('Do you think . . . ?', 'Do you not think . . . ?').

After the lesson I said to the teacher, 'You clearly had an interpretation of that scene that you wanted to teach them. Why didn't you just tell them what it was?' Interesting, his reply was, 'I didn't want to force it on them.' I pointed out that, if that was what he was concerned about, he could have presented his interpretation as a hypothesis and then invited the pupils to test it and try to improve or replace it. I also said that I was sure that the pupils knew that the teacher had an interpretation that he wanted them to get to and that they were simply trying to double-guess it. Had the teacher presented his interpretation through a short session of chalk-and-talk, it would have been (a) clearer and (b) quicker.

I tell this anecdote because of its typicality. There are two morals to be drawn:

1 If you write 'Question-and-answer' in your lesson plan, ensure the questions are genuine (see Idea 63). Avoid pseudo-questions.
2 If you have an argument that you want to explain, there's no need to be shy of straightforward presentation.

One simple way to turn passive learning into active is to ask pupils to process the items that they are learning about into categories. Tell them that, as they listen or read, they need to put each item (idea, fact, statement or whatever) into certain pre-ordained categories. Examples of categorising systems include:

○ Binary opposites (e.g. true/false, for/against).
○ Trinities. Edward de Bono has suggested, for example, that instead of simply sorting ideas into 'Positive' or 'Negative' we liberate our thinking by adding 'Interesting' as a third category.
○ Quadrants constructed from two axes. For example, political beliefs and policies are often rated on two scales – conservative/radical and authoritarian/democratic.

Systems with more than four categories tend to require more thought and almost certainly need to be used as exercises *after* pupils have read or listened to material.

Though sorting activities can be used at various points of the lesson, they are particularly useful at the start as a way of getting pupils actively engaged. After a sorting activity has been completed individually or in pairs, pupils can then work in groups to compare and debate their decisions.

Scoring activities are those that require pupils to rank or evaluate the items they are learning about. Like sorting activities (Idea 65), they are a simple way of transforming passive into active learning. Pupils listen to or read some material and then assign an explicit value or rank to each item (statement, example, etc.) that they encounter.

Here are some common formats.

1 A five-point scale for expressing agreement or attraction:

++ / + / 0 / − / − −.

Pupils agreeing strongly with a statement, for example, draw a ring round '++'.

Those disagreeing to some extent ring '−'. '0' stands for a neutral response.

2 A page consisting of empty boxes in the shape of a pyramid (one box on the top line, two on the next, and so on). Pupils write the item they rate highest in the box on the top line, the two items they rate next highest in the boxes on the second line, and so on. An alternative structure is a diamond.

3 Pupils are given a certain number of points to award. They award the points in proportion to their evaluations. They can spread the points as evenly or unevenly as they wish, although you can encourage decisiveness by ensuring that the number of points to be awarded is not divisible by the number of items to be evaluated.

Scoring activities can be used at various points of a lesson. For example, a scoring activity performed individually or in pairs can form a useful fulcrum between a receptive activity, such as reading or listening to material, and a group or class discussion. Scoring activities can be useful too at the end of lessons as a way of encouraging pupils to arrive at informed judgements or decisions (see Idea 23) about what they have learnt.

Imagine a class discussion on the causes of unemployment:

> *Pupil A: One reason for unemployment is that the*
> *unemployed do not have enough skills to offer.*
> *Pupil B: A more important reason is that*
> *unemployment benefit is too high.*

Now imagine Pupil A says one of the following:

1 'You can't say it's all caused by unemployment benefit.'
2 'You can't say that poor skills aren't a cause [or don't matter].'

Statements (1) or (2) may very well be true (whether or not they are depends on empirical fact). Neither, however, constitutes a refutation of Pupil B's assertion. That assertion was a comparative statement – that one cause was 'more important' – not an absolute or exclusive one.

This kind of (fallacious) argument is fairly standard for such discussion in class (and anywhere else, I reckon!). Logic is very important in learning, yet we tend to require pupils to be logical without doing much to teach it. This is like expecting people to play chess without telling them the rules.

There are various resources we can use to plan teaching of logic. My favourite – as a resource for teachers themselves – is Madsen Pirie's *How to Win Every Argument*. Where in your plans does logic come?

Edward de Bono argues that we use two types of thinking – vertical thinking and lateral thinking. Among the differences between them that he identifies are the following:

Vertical thinking	Lateral thinking
Is sequential	Makes jumps
Selects ideas	Generates ideas
Analyses ideas	Provokes ideas
Has to be correct at every stage	Does not have to be correct at every stage

Though it can be fun to use lateral thinking exercises as fillers (see Idea 74), it is also useful to train pupils to use lateral thinking in your subject. For example, one technique that I've found useful is what de Bono calls 'the generation of alternatives'. This involves taking an idea or problem and seeing how many ways you can find for restating it. Rather than dismissing each restatement as just 'saying the same thing', one welcomes each new nuance for its potential to trigger a new idea or solution. Try it with a problem such as 'being late for school'.

I recommend starting with de Bono's own book, *Lateral Thinking*, which is packed with ideas and examples (both verbal and visual), straightforwardly expressed and divided into bite-sized chunks.

LATERAL THINKING

M TRAPS DAVE

When you use the perfect tense of a verb in French, you need to combine the verb with another – either 'avoir' or 'être'. The man who taught me French gave me a mnemonic so that I could remember which verbs combined with 'être'. As a tribute to him I've used it as the title for this page. Each letter stands for the first letter of one of the verbs I needed to remember (the 'e', for example, stands for 'entrer').

There are several interesting features about mnemonics. First, they are extraordinarily effective. People sometimes remember them for the rest of their lives. Second, everyone seems to like them, form attachments and loyalties to them – and feels grateful to whoever provides them. Third, the odder they are, the better they seem to work (what on earth, after all does 'M TRAPS DAVE' mean?)

Prepare mnemonics for things you want to teach your pupils to remember. Even better, try writing one on the board, unexplained, at the start of the lesson and then gradually explain what it stands for as the lesson progresses.

Asking pupils to research something can be a great idea, but sometimes ends in frustration. Pupil researchers often start to feel swamped with information and (to switch metaphors) end up being unable to see the wood for the trees. They need a method. The following is serviceable and adaptable, though you might want to reduce the number of stages:

1 Define what you want to find out.
2 Discover what resources are available.
3 Decide which of these you are going to use.
4 Locate/retrieve them.
5 Study the resources.
6 Make notes/record information.
7 Bring together/sort out your findings.
8 Summarize.
9 Evaluate your findings.
10 Present your report.

PUPIL RESEARCH

IDEA

71

CHECKING

If you encourage pupils to check their work, you will help them to improve its quality and also teach them a valuable life skill. But it requires more than simply saying, 'Have you checked it?' before you take in work. You need to allow time to (a) teach pupils how to check work and (b) allow them to do it properly.

In teaching pupils how to check work, you might be able to draw on particular techniques or problem areas in your subject area. For example, assessment criteria in humanities sometimes require pupils to list their sources so asking pupils to check that they have done so is an obvious strategy. But as well as particularities, it is important to teach constructive attitudes such as (a) checking is an integral part of the learning process, (b) recognizing that there will be errors or omissions awaiting attention, and (c) checking pays – it improves the quality of your work.

It is important to allow time in your plan for proper checking. A 'quick check' is almost a contradiction in terms. Note that the best time for checking is not usually straight after the completion of a task. Consider giving the work back, unmarked, in the next lesson (perhaps at the start) for checking then.

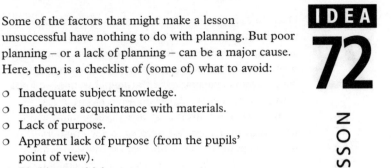

Some of the factors that might make a lesson unsuccessful have nothing to do with planning. But poor planning – or a lack of planning – can be a major cause. Here, then, is a checklist of (some of) what to avoid:

o   Inadequate subject knowledge.
o   Inadequate acquaintance with materials.
o   Lack of purpose.
o   Apparent lack of purpose (from the pupils' point of view).
o   Pitching too high.
o   Pitching too low.
o   Inappropriate pace.
o   Poor time management.
o   Work unrelated to other lessons.
o   Failure to draw on pupils' prior knowledge or experience.
o   Appealing only to very limited range of learning styles.
o   Lack of differentiation.
o   Undefined or inappropriate expectations.
o   Opaque language.

WHAT MAKES A BAD LESSON

JUST DO IT

Over the last couple of decades, schools have become more managerial in their ethos. We have become generally more interested in such matters as specifying objectives and reviewing practice. More lessons begin with teachers explaining the learning objectives and end with plenary sessions reviewing what has been learnt.

In many ways this is a positive development, which is why much of this book is devoted to such matters. But I worry when pragmatic principles get transformed into creeds. The fact that such methods are generally Good Things does not mean that you *have* to do them *every time* – despite what school inspectorates may pretend.

I remember what was possibly the best – and certainly the most memorable – lesson I have taught. It was one in which literally nobody said a single word at any point. The (often far from angelic) class arrived for the private-reading lesson that we always had on Friday mornings. They sat down. They got out their books. They started reading. So did I. When the bell went, I grinned, they packed their bags and we waved each other goodbye.

Had there, unbeknown to me, been an inspector in the corner and had s/he asked whether the learning objectives had been met or requested evidence of the pupils' progress, I would have been in difficulty. But I tell you, it was a great lesson.

Sometimes, just do it.

Good planning rather removes the need for filler activities, but they still tend to be useful every now and then – for example, when a colleague is delayed and you're asked to cover the class for a while.

Word games, lateral thinking exercises (see Idea 68), mathematical puzzles and Sudoku are all candidates. Hangman and twenty questions are passable, but rather tired, games. Books such as *The Penguin Book of Word Games* and Martin Gardner's various collections of mathematical puzzles are useful resources to obtain and keep handy.

Here are a few of my favourites, ranging from the basic to the more complex.

1 The opposite of free association. A pupil says a word. The next pupil has to say a word that has nothing to do with the previous word. The third pupil may do likewise, but if s/he feels that the previous word does in fact have some connection with the word before that, may instead challenge. The challenger then has to explain the connection. You, as umpire, have to decide if the challenge is plausible. This game only works if played at a high pace.

2 Kolodny's Game. The point of the game is to discover the rule that one of the players has formulated. Someone is chosen as respondent (sometimes it's good to use a pair of pupils so that they can check each other's answers). They have to answer questions with either yes or no. The answer depends not on the content of the question but on its form. For example, if the respondent decides that the rule is to answer yes to questions beginning with a vowel and no to those beginning with a consonant, then the answer to 'Can you see the sun?' is no but the answer to 'Is the sun visible?' is yes.

3 I don't know what this one is called. Divide pupils into two teams. The first player, representing Team A, writes a three-letter word. Its score depends on the position of the letters of the alphabet (e.g. A = 1): so AGE = 9 (1 + 7 + 5). The next player, representing Team B, must contribute a three-letter word beginning with the last letter of the previous one, for

example EAT (= 26). Keep a cumulative score (35 so far i.e. 9 + 26). Continue to alternate between teams. When one team contributes a word that causes the total to reach one of a number of pre-announced figures (e.g. 113), the other team scores a point. A (harder) variant is to forget the totals but require each word contributed to score more highly than the previous one.

Homework can be a minefield. Pupils don't do it, or they don't do it very well, or they leave it at home or . . . There are enough problems without allowing the actual *setting* of it to become one too – yet this is all too easy. Consider, for example, this far from uncommon scenario. The teacher thinks, 'I'll set the homework at the end of the lesson.' Something crops up, takes the teacher's attention for a couple of minutes. Suddenly there's no time left. The teacher rushes the explanation. The pupils are anxious to catch the bus. They aren't listening carefully. Some of them get confused and ask questions. The rest are packing their books instead of writing down the instructions. The lesson ends with a hassled teacher and confused pupils. When the next lesson comes the pupils haven't done the homework because they 'didn't get it'.

This is a classic case of needing to allocate time better. As suggested in Idea 78, a mental rehearsal when planning the lesson helps. When you write 'Set homework' on your plan, remember you need to allow time to:

o state the homework;
o explain it;
o field questions;
o check that pupils have understood the task;
o get pupils to write the homework instructions down;
o check that pupils have written them down – and accurately;
o hand out any resources needed.

On your plan it may well be better to write '5–10 mins' than '2 mins'. And it will usually be better not to leave it to the end of the lesson. Could it even be done at the start?

VARIETIES OF HOMEWORK

It is natural to use homework for 'finishing off', but natural is not always best. Setting 'finishing off' homeworks can cause problems, especially if you do so repeatedly. For example:

○ It can have the effect of penalising both the slowest and the most thorough.
○ It can reduce effort in class ('I can always do it later').
○ It can reduce pupils' decision-making over how they approach tasks (the more time-limited a task is, the more they have to decide where to focus).
○ It can become a dull routine.

Ring the changes. Set, for example, parallel tasks that provide further (but fresh) practice for the skill learnt in class, or sequels, or a new task designed to move the skill to a higher level.

I've always been intrigued by the fact that in independent schools pupils tend to refer not to 'homework' but to 'prep'. Homework as 'preparation' rather than 'finishing off' raises interesting possibilities of pupils generating ideas, researching information, collecting resources – with the advantage that they might provide refreshing contributions to the next lesson. By donating resources (e.g. news cuttings), students start to feel some ownership of the lesson. They become, as the modern jargon has it, stakeholders.

Homeworks involving thinking, research and so on often do not involve much writing, if any, and for that reason can be difficult to monitor. But it is important not to let the tail wag the dog – and the thought occurs that not being able to monitor (or mark) a homework occasionally might be a good thing!

Providing teachers with support staff is very expensive. It can also be very productive – but isn't necessarily so. If you're in the fortunate position of having some support, it's important to devote some thought to how to use it.

Seek to develop a constructive relationship based on mutual respect. Acknowledge good practice. Involve support staff in your planning by sharing plans and materials before the lesson and by soliciting contributions to the planning process.

Consider the roles in which you want to use support staff. Much time might be taken up with ancillary work, such as setting up equipment, and supporting selected individual pupils. Such work may be useful, even necessary. But note that having another adult in the room provides an extra voice to draw on (see Idea 37). Sometimes, too, it's possible to do things with two adults that couldn't be done with one. For example, when my daughter was at primary school her class studied Mexico. Her teacher and the teaching assistant asked the class to imagine flying to Mexico. They set out the chairs in rows as in an aeroplane and adopted the roles of pilot and flight attendant. It didn't take long, but evidently captured the pupils' imagination.

Support staff can contribute constructive observations about your pupils and your lessons, especially if you make it clear that they are welcome to do so. You can, too, ask them to observe particular points (see Idea 94).

Three big issues

GETTING THE TIMING RIGHT

Experience of working with inexperienced teachers – trainees, for example, and newly-qualified staff – suggests that one of most common pitfalls of lesson planning is wrongly estimating the time that some activity will take.

We've all been there. Pupils finish in ten minutes a task that you allowed half an hour for. Or you realize towards the end of a forty-five minute lesson that you still haven't finished the introduction that was supposed to take ten minutes.

The main solution is simply experience – the more you teach, the more you develop a feel for how long various activities take. But there is one particular technique that will help. This is to mentally rehearse each part of the lesson you're planning to deliver.

I don't mean rehearse roughly, I mean do it minutely. You plan to give out some books: right, what does that involve? Where are they kept? If they're in a locked cupboard, allow time to unlock the cupboard. Who will give them out? How long will that take? By thinking through each process you can alert yourself to places in your plan where you might have allowed either too much time or too little. It helps in addition not to write a single estimated time against each activity but a maximum and minimum – so against 'pair work', for example, you write not '10 mins' but, say, '5–15 mins'.

Pitch a lesson too low and pupils will feel bored. Pitch it too high and they will feel discouraged. Learning to pitch a lesson just right is a difficult art – one that usually requires experience to master.

Something that helps, however, is to get used to assessing the readability of materials. If you make regular use of the methods outlined in Idea 88 for assessing written materials, you will find that, as if by osmosis, the awareness that you develop will transfer across. You will get better at gauging the pitch of both your instruction to the class and the tasks you set.

I should add that I've often found that trainees who have only just graduated tend to pitch lessons too high. If you are a trainee, try preparing part of a lesson at the level that you judge appropriate, then bring it down one level – and then ask yourself whether it might be better to come down one level further.

GETTING THE PITCH RIGHT

EXPECTATIONS

In listing the headings for the Perfect Plan (see Appendix) I did not include 'Expectations'. Expectations are difficult to summarize in a document. The level of expectation is, however, important. Unless you have decided it in advance, you can end up in the lesson feeling hopelessly at sea. You have set a task – discussing the language of a story, say – and you are aware that the level at which the pupils are performing the task is not what you expected, but then you realize that you don't have any clear idea of what it is you were expecting. The point is that, until you have a clear idea in your own mind, you will not convey one to the pupils. After all, without some indication of expectation from you, most of our instructions are ambiguous: 'Write a report', for example, is an instruction that can be fulfilled in a variety of ways at a variety of levels.

Though you might not include a statement of expectations in your formal plan, it does help to consider the matter at least informally. You may find it helps in preparing a lesson to dramatize it a little in your head.

In trying to set the level of expectation at the optimal level for your pupils, think of them as people who see a bus coming. If they're already waiting at the bus stop, or very near, they won't do much running – they know they'll catch the bus anyway. They won't bother running either if they're a long way from the stop – they know they won't catch it. They need to be fairly near to really stretch themselves.

After the lesson

KEEPING RECORDS OF YOUR PLANS

You keep some forms of records automatically – pupils' attendance, for example, and the marks they achieve. But it is worth also keeping a record of the plan itself. I suggest keeping the original plan and annotating it – in either a different colour or font. Annotations may be very brief. For example, you might tick the date at the top of your plan to show that you did indeed deliver the lesson on the day you planned it for. You can note aspects of the context that affected the lesson – pupils arriving late from another lesson, for example, or the wind and rain outside making the pupils 'high'. In particular, jot down things that didn't go quite according to plan – an instruction being misunderstood, for example.

Such records are useful for the purpose of accountability. But they will also help you the next time you want to teach that lesson. They will bring the previous occasion back to life for you and help you to decide whether and how to modify your plan.

Maybe it's a matter of taste, but I have always preferred to do this on paper rather than on screen. Annotating the printout of your plan can be done straightaway, is quicker than logging back in, and seems somehow to encourage an informal approach – which makes it more likely that you'll get round to doing it.

If you have formulated learning objectives for your lesson you will be unsurprised to hear that the first stage of evaluation is to assess the extent to which your objectives were achieved. Sometimes this can be done with a simple tick or cross. Often it's more complex than that – pupils got part of the way to an objective, for example, or some did better than others. It's worth trying briefly to quantify the outcome – 17 out of 30 pupils got the right answer, say, or 25 improved their grades.

The second stage of evaluation is less obvious. As explained in Idea 15, learning objectives are not all-important. Valuable forms of learning can occur beyond the objectives you set. Ask yourself, therefore, what *else* of value or interest occurred other than the learning specified by your objectives?

TWO-STEP APPROACH TO EVALUATION

DETAILED EVALUATION

It can be helpful to construct a standard questionnaire for your own use when evaluating your lessons. You might ask yourself questions such as:

1 How well did the pupils understand the objectives?
2 How clearly did they understand my instructions?
3 How quickly did we get working?
4 How well did I allocate time?
5 How well did I pitch the material?
6 How adequate were the resources I used?
7 To what extent were my expectations satisfied?
8 How clear were the outcomes?
9 What are the implications for the next time I teach this lesson?

No teacher is going to use such a questionnaire for every lesson, but it can be useful to do so at least occasionally as a form of 'clinic'. After a while you may find, as I have done, that particular areas for development in your teaching emerge. In this case, it helps to construct a questionnaire consisting of just two or three questions focused on the key areas and then to apply the questionnaire systematically.

Detailed evaluation of your lesson planning (see Idea 83) is all very well, but it takes time – and life is short. And, in any case, sometimes the very detail results in your not seeing the wood for the trees. Sometimes it is better to stand back and ask yourself just one question, that is, 'What's the single biggest point that strikes me about that lesson?'

I dare say that inspectors, teacher educators, principals and so on may suck their teeth and say that this is not a rigorous form of evaluation. I've found it works rather like a sorbet in the middle of a rich meal – it's very simple and is wonderfully cleansing.

BROAD-BRUSH EVALUATION

REVIEW

Ideas 82–84 deal with the evaluation of lesson plans. Evaluation is all well and good, but it is only actually useful if it is accompanied by a review. By review I mean literally a 're-view', i.e. looking again at something. The reviewing process is when you decide, in the light of your evaluation, which aspects of your plans, if any, to change. I suggest a three-step approach.

First, review the implications for your next lesson with the same class. If, for example, you feel that the lesson did not achieve its objectives, you may need to revise work before moving on to the next stage in the scheme of work. It is also helpful to review more general aspects: were the pace and pitch, for example, right for this class?

Second, review the implications for the next time you teach the same lesson, which may well be next year. It's best to do this, and to note your decisions, as soon as possible, before your memory fades – otherwise each year becomes merely a rerun of the previous one.

Third, review your teaching not just of this lesson or class, but in general. Ask yourself questions about your approach and the form that lessons take. For example, are you setting objectives that are achievable (Idea 12)? How well are you analysing the tasks that you set (Idea 50)? Are you allowing enough time to set homework properly (Idea 75)?

SECTION
9

Resources

IDEA 86

In many parts of the world, textbooks are regarded as a major resource for teaching. In Britain, they tend to get a bad press. Many teacher trainers seem to ignore or even disapprove of them. Textbooks are associated with heavily didactic, even authoritarian pedagogy and boring, passive learning.

It would be a shame to ignore the potential of textbooks. Some are well designed and intelligently written – and even the less good ones can serve as useful sources. Some of the alternatives – hurriedly produced handouts, for example – are not obviously better!

Much depends on how textbooks are used. They can be used monotonously and uncritically, but do not have to be. Consider using textbooks as follows:

○ As a resource bank into which you can dip with pupils to read particular passages, tables, charts, etc.
○ As a source, like any other source, to be discussed, assessed and criticized.
○ For comparison and contrast: juxtaposing two textbook accounts of a common topic provides a straightforward, concrete way to demonstrate how knowledge in your subject can be constructed in more than one way.

If you are going to design your own materials, take the word 'design' seriously. That is, attend to the visual aspects – the layout, font, and so on. Design matters for two reasons. First, clear, attractive resources will be more effective. Second, you will be providing a good model for pupils. Shoddy design – misnumbering of questions, for example – is obviously unacceptable. The problem, however, is usually not that the design is shoddy, but rather that it is inert.

Exploit the following basic principles of good design:

1   Items that are related to each other need to be brought together on the page. For example, if you are designing a test paper, use one part of the page for the rubric and keep its elements (how many questions to do, whether to start each question on a new sheet, etc.) as close to each other as possible.
2   If there are differences between items, accentuate those differences by using bold contrast. (In the above example, make the rubric look mind-blowingly different from the test questions.) Audacious use of contrast not only makes documents more navigable, it also makes them more striking and captures attention.
3   Develop a design style within and between materials. One colleague developed his own logo – a drawing of a pig, always placed bottom right. Whenever a teacher in his department gave out a worksheet, the pupils would look straightaway to see if it had a pig on it. Trivial – but it shows the power of repetition. Consider using as your standard font something other than Times New Roman – it will make your documents look fresh.

For a wonderfully entertaining and practical introductory guide to good design, see Robin Williams, *The Non-Designer's Design Book*.

ASSESSING READABILITY

It is obviously useful to assess the readability of materials before you use them in class. I suggest two approaches.

First, there is the informal approach. Look at the material that you are planning to use (or, in the case of a lengthy text, selected passages from it) and ask yourself:

1 What conceptual or logical difficulties is it likely to present?
2 What verbal difficulties (e.g. unfamiliar words) is it likely to present?
3 What grammatical difficulties (e.g. complex sentence structures) is it likely to present?
4 How does the design and typography make the material more or less readable?

Second, there is the formal approach, using quantitative techniques such as the Flesch Scale or the Fry Graph. Such techniques, which are readily Google-able, depend on the assumptions that:

○ polysyllabic words are harder to read than short ones;
○ long sentences are harder to read than shorter ones.

Though such assumptions do not always hold, they are at least commonsensical. Such techniques produce a readability score, enabling you to compare texts.

The best way to assess readability is usually to employ informal *and* formal methods.

It's easy to set questions, but difficult to set them well.
Here's a five-step guide.

1 Clarify your purpose(s) for setting questions. For
   example, it may be to:
   o encourage pupils to revisit material;
   o encourage them to check their understanding;
   o develop their understanding further;
   o encourage them to transfer or apply their
     knowledge;
   o enable you to assess your pupils' learning;
   o provide pupils with experience of examination
     questions.

2 It's easy to limit the range of questions by restricting
   yourself unwittingly to a narrow range of
   interrogatives. Seek to use as many of the following as
   possible: Who? (Whom?), What?, When? (Whence?
   Whither?), Where?, Which?, How?, Why?

3 Examine the type of questions you set by asking
   yourself whether the balance between open (e.g. 'How
   far do you agree that . . . ?') and closed questions
   (e.g. 'Do you agree that . . . ?') is right. Do you need
   to convert some of the closed questions into open
   ones?

4 Try to step questions in order of complexity or
   difficulty. This not only guides pupils and builds their
   confidence, but also makes it easier for you to assess
   what level they are working at. One way to do this
   is to begin with recall questions, then move on to
   inferential questions, and finish with application
   questions.

5 Finally, you can review the range of your questioning
   by asking yourself (where applicable) whether you
   have included questions about:
   o the big picture (the wood) *and* the detail
     (the trees)?
   o similarities *and* differences?
   o the past, present *and* future?
   o people, objects *and* processes?

PREPARING QUESTION SHEETS

MAKE YOUR LESSON PLANS VISUAL

You may think that the following point is too basic to need making. Working with trainee teachers especially has convinced me otherwise. The point is simply that you need to write your lesson plan so that you can refer to it at a glance. It's all too easy to lose momentum, and eye contact, by pausing to pore over a minuscule point in your plan. The irony is that the more carefully you plan your lessons, the more likely they are to be undone by over-detailed notes.

It helps to use diagrammatic forms, for example, a box for each phase of the lesson. Use large font – and highlighter pen. Or, as people often do when giving speeches, use a series of prompt cards, each with a key phrase on it. With one difficult class I experimented by pinning key words on the back wall of the classroom – I could then remind myself of the lesson plan without taking my eyes off the class.

If you enjoy creating resources and also enjoy collecting resources – the postcard or news cutting that might prove useful, the worksheet you pinched from a colleague at your previous school – you will soon find that you have more resources than you can remember. It can be very frustrating to discover, just *after* you've taught a topic, that you had in your cupboard the perfect resource.

It pays, therefore, to keep a simple index. My own system consists of the following columns:

○ Content: a key word or two to say what the resource is about.
○ Curriculum area(s) that the resource belongs to (e.g. History: Romans).
○ The level at which you expect to use it.
○ The location you keep it in (e.g. folder name).

There are countless lessons plans available on the Internet. Sites such as TeacherNet (www.teachernet. gov.uk), LessonPlansPage.com (www.lessonplanspage. com) and Lesson Planet (www.lessonplanet.com) provide thousands.

The good news is that you need never be short of ideas – a few clicks will enable you to borrow from other teachers. The bad news is that this will not get you very far down the road of professional planning. If you look (again) at Ideas 2–8, 29–30, 33 and 85 you will see why I say that.

A lesson simply lifted off the Internet and delivered unmediated to your pupils might do a job for you in certain circumstances – it might, for example, plug a sudden gap in your planning. But to benefit any more than that you are likely to have to adapt the lesson plan to your own style and context, embed it in your medium-term planning, differentiate it to meet the needs of your pupils, supplement it with appropriate objectives – do, in other words, what teachers have traditionally been very good at, namely both borrowing *and* transforming.

My suggestion, therefore, is to see lesson plan websites as a catalyst for your own creativity rather than a substitute for it.

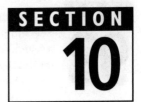

Development

In 2000 the Department for Education and Skills in England published the Hay McBer model based on research it had commissioned into effective teaching (see the TeacherNet website: www.teachernet.gov.uk). The research estimated that 30% of variance in pupil progress was attributable to teachers' professional characteristics, their teaching skills, and the climate of their classrooms.

The model included planning and the setting of expectations in its list of professional characteristics. It stressed a need for:

o 'energy in setting and meeting challenging targets';
o 'intellectual curiosity';
o the willingness to 'anticipate and pre-empt events'.

The Hay McBer model also included aspects of planning in relation to teaching skills. Among the key skills listed are:

o not only having a clear plan and clear objectives, but also communicating them at the beginnings of lessons;
o having the necessary teaching and learning resources ready for the lesson;
o reviewing at the end of the lesson what pupils have learnt.

None of this is particularly novel, but then (to paraphrase Dr Johnson) sometimes we need to be reminded rather than informed. Use the points listed above (six in total) as a checklist for ensuring professionalism in your planning.

Idea 93 draws on one research project on teacher effectiveness. I'd love to point you in the direction of all kinds of additional research findings concerning lesson planning, but I can't. I've searched various research databases and come to the conclusion that the subject – despite forming one of the staples of teaching – is seriously under-researched. But you can at least research your own classroom.

If you ever have another adult – a teaching assistant, for example – in your own classroom, you can ask them to observe aspects of the lesson for you. In particular, they can observe the lesson to see how the reality compared to your plan. Then you can learn to adjust your planning in future.

Observation works best when you specify something precise and easy to judge – preferably something that relates to a concern that you have. The classic example – and one of the most useful – is recording a time log to show how long each activity or phase of the lesson actually took.

EVIDENCE-INFORMED LESSON PLANNING

Usually there is a gap of several years between one's own schooling and starting work as a teacher oneself. As a result it's easy to let memories of being taught fade away. When it comes to lesson planning, however, memory can be a useful resource.

I've found it helpful to recall how the best of the teachers who taught me went about the business. I remember one teacher who was successful with class discussion and good at getting pupils involved. Thinking back over those lessons makes me think that this had something to do with the irregular arrangement of furniture in the room – different seating positions leant themselves to different roles in discussion – and also with the telling of sort-of relevant jokes and anecdotes.

Some of the ideas in this book – 61 and 86, for example – had their genesis in my learning from teachers as a pupil. I've found it less rewarding to reflect on unsuccessful teachers – usually the reasons for their lack of success were pretty obvious.

Working out the elements behind your teachers' success doesn't mean, of course, that you can adopt those elements lock, stock and barrel – there are important questions of style (see Idea 5) and context (Idea 4) to consider. However, it does at least help to expand the range of approaches that you can draw on in your planning.

You may well teach a thousand lessons each year. However committed and conscientious you are, there is a danger of getting stuck in your ways, ground down by routine or just bored. One way to prevent this is by deliberately doing the opposite of what you usually do.

In *Developing Materials for Language Teaching* (edited by Brian Tomlinson), Alan Maley recommends occasionally doing the opposite in terms of 'content, process, roles':

> *If you habitually use written texts, try using listening instead. If you use long texts, try short ones. If you use simplified texts, use authentic ones . . . If you use a lot of group and pair work, try some individual and whole class work . . . If you do all the teaching, let the students do some of it. If you set tests, let students write their own.* (p. 188)

Though Maley is writing for teachers of ELT, his advice is easy to adapt for other subjects.

REVERSAL

Researching this book brought home to me how little help is available to teachers on this subject. The general textbooks on teaching tend, in my opinion, to cover lesson planning rather vaguely and superficially. Showing trainee teachers a pro forma comprising boxes with such labels as 'objectives' and 'evaluation', for example (as many such books do), is not much use without some detailed discussion of the meaning and purpose of each item and how to go about formulating the information required.

There are two books specifically on lesson planning that I like. *Lesson Planning* by Graham Butt (published by Continuum) has become well known and is widely available, at least in the UK. It is practical, concise and accessible and covers many aspects of the subject that other books omit, for example, problem areas. The book benefits throughout from the author's use of realistic examples.

As the title implies, K. Paul Kasambira's *Lesson Planning and Class Management* (Longman) deals not only with lesson planning but also with some other practical aspects of teaching. The book is detailed and very clearly organized. It too benefits from plentiful examples. Written by a teacher trainer in America who has taught in primary and secondary schools in Zimbabwe, the book is less rooted in British education systems than is Graham Butt's.

I recommend both books strongly. Although there is, inevitably, some overlap with the book you're reading now, both of the above will supplement this book with their own perspectives and a consideration of some details that I've decided to omit.

This idea contradicts itself. On the one hand, I want to suggest that you detach your time outside school from your lesson planning. The danger, if you are a resourceful teacher, is that it becomes impossible to stop thinking about the job. Unless you are careful, every time you pick up the newspaper you will find yourself thinking, 'I can use this in school!' – and perhaps you can, but that doesn't help you recharge your batteries. I think I started to find some activities – playing boules or croquet, for example – absorbing precisely because I could see no link to my teaching. Although if I think about them long enough . . .

But I also want to suggest that in one way you use your own time to inform your lesson planning. On several occasions I found that becoming a pupil again myself made me think more carefully about my lessons. For example, I learnt to drive a couple of years after I started teaching. I also once attended parttime over several months an excellent course on teaching bilingual pupils. Such experiences reminded me that in discussion, whatever the subject matter, the question of what other people – the teacher, other students – were thinking was never far from the front of my mind. I know I wasn't the only one.

Bizarre though it might sound, I can recommend experiencing for yourself at least once some bad teaching or coaching. I went on two poorly prepared short courses on certain aspects of teaching. Both occasions served to remind me how *not* to plan lessons – though I think one would have been enough!

LESSON PLANNING AND
YOUR SELF-DEVELOPMENT

PUBLISH YOUR LESSON PLANS

You can publish your lesson plans in several ways – on the Internet (see Idea 92), in resource packs, or in discursive books. There are several reasons why this is worth considering. First, altruism – if you have developed some approaches that work it will help the profession if you share them. Second, direct earnings – don't expect to give up the day job, but your royalties might enable you to have a better summer holiday. Third, indirect earnings – authors often get asked to do other forms of writing, give talks, etc. – and the earnings from these may be greater than the original royalty. Fourth, kudos and perhaps even career development – publication enhances your reputation among colleagues in the staffroom or your subject association, and looks good on the CV. Fifth, in the process of publishing material the author usually improves it a little. This will benefit your own teaching in due course.

Educational publishing depends largely on economies of scale. Publishers, for example, like to be able to cross-market their titles. It is usually in everyone's interest, therefore, if the publisher you approach is one that already publishes into the market your proposed publication is aimed at. In selecting a publisher to approach, therefore, start by looking at who published the titles on your (and your colleagues') shelves. Look for a series that your publication could slot into.

Most publishers specify on their websites what form they wish to receive publication proposals in. If they don't, write an outline specifying the title, content, market, need, sales angles and opportunities, your qualities, qualifications and affiliation, schedule, the length of the text and any illustration or special design features required. If possible, include some sample material (carefully checked) and endorsements from people in the profession. Find out the name of the commissioning editor and address the envelope and covering letter to that person. Include your name and contact details, enclose an SAE and retain a copy of your proposal.

This book as a whole is concerned with ways to develop the best possible plan for each lesson. There are, however, two ways to move beyond this idea.

First, you can allow the class to choose their own adventure. When planning lessons, we often find that various alternatives present themselves. There is, after all, more than one way to skin a cat. Usually as teachers we weigh up the alternatives, select the one we prefer and discard the others. But there is, of course, another option, which is to invite the class to decide: 'There are two ways in which we can cover this topic and I'd like you to decide which way we should go.'

Second, you can abandon a plan. Sometimes this is necessary just because the original plan clearly isn't working. A more positive reason is simply that something more interesting turns up. You cannot predict everything that will occur in a lesson. Sometimes an unexpected comment or question opens up a more interesting horizon than the one you were heading for.

Recently I prepared for a group of adults a carefully structured session about writing skills. At the start I said, 'Before we begin, can you tell me of any questions about writing that you want me to cover during this session?' I received something like a dozen questions, many of them wide ranging and thought provoking. I said, 'Let me see if I can deal with some of them before we move on to the material I've brought with me.' We ended up devoting the entire session to discussing those questions. We did use some of the material I'd prepared, but none of it in the sequence I'd planned.

One of the benefits of planning a route is that you've got something to detour from.

THE PERFECT PLAN

The perfect plan will include information on the following:

1 Aims
2 Objectives and learning outcomes
3 Assessment data on pupils
4 Scope and content
5 Pedagogical methods
6 Teacher's expectations
7 Learning activities
8 Homework
9 Differentiation of learning
10 Progression in learning
11 Other curricular links
12 Resources
13 Ancillary staff
14 Risks
15 Assessment
16 Evaluation method(s)
17 Review procedure(s).

REFERENCES

Edward de Bono, *Lateral Thinking* (Penguin, 1990).

Graham Butt, *Lesson Planning* 2nd edn. (Continuum, 2006).

Tony Cline & Norah Frederickson, *Curriculum Related Assessment, Cummins and Bilingual Children* (Multilingual Matters, 1996).

Kieran Egan, *Teaching as Story Telling* (Routledge, 1988).

Graham Gibbs, *53 Interesting things to do in your seminars and tutorials* (Technical and Educational Services, 1984).

E.D. Hirsch, *Cultural Literacy* (Houghton Mifflin, 1987)

Alan Howe, *Expanding Horizons* (NATE, 1988).

K. Paul Kasambira, *Lesson Planning and Class Management* (Longman, 1993).

Manuel Martinez-Pons, *The Psychology of Teaching and Learning* (Continuum, 2001).

David Parlett, *The Penguin Book of Word Games* (Harmondsworth, 1981).

Madsen Pirie, *How to Win Every Argument* (Continuum, 2006).

Brian Tomlinson (ed.), *Developing Materials for Language Teaching* (Continuum, 2003).

Robin Williams, *The Non-Designer's Design Book* 2nd edn. (Peachpit Press, 2004).

Report of the Committee of Inquiry into the Teaching of English Language (HMSO, 1988).